ELEMENTS OF *Wri...*

MW01268316

PRACTICE
for
ASSESSMENT

- •READING
- •VOCABULARY
- •SPELLING

WORKSHEETS AND PRACTICE TESTS

WITH TEACHING NOTES AND ANSWER KEYS

▶ First Course

HOLT, RINEHART AND WINSTON
Harcourt Brace & Company
Austin • *New York* • *Orlando* • *Atlanta* • *San Francisco* • *Boston* • *Dallas* • *Toronto* • *London*

Staff Credits

Associate Director: Mescal Evler

Managing Editor: Steve Welch

Senior Editor: Charlene L. Rodgers

Editorial Staff: *Editors,* Julie V. Barnett, Ed Combs, Robyn Stuart Czarnecki, Teresa Diaz, Colleen Hobbs; *Copy Editors,* Atietie O. Tonwe, Senior Copyeditor; Joseph S. Schofield IV; *Coordinators,* Amanda F. Beard, Senior Editorial Coordinator; Susan G. Alexander, Rebecca Bennett, Wendy Langabeer, Marie Hoffman Price; *Support,* Ruth A. Hooker, Senior Word Processor; Kelly Keeley, Margaret Sanchez, Pat Stover

Design: Christine Schueler

Editorial Permissions: Janet Harrington

Production Coordinator: Rosa Mayo Degollado

Electronic Publishing Supervisor: Barbara Hudgens

Electronic Publishing Staff: Heather Jernt, *Project Coordinator*
JoAnn Brown, Rina May Ouellette, Michele Ruschhaupt, Charlie Taliaferro, Ethan Thompson

Contributing Writer

John Roberts

ISBN 0-03-051149-6

1 2 3 4 5 085 00 99 98 97

Contents

To the Teacher

The teacher support provided by the *Annotated Teacher's Edition* is further reinforced by the *Teaching Resources.*

Practice for Assessment in Reading, Vocabulary, and Spelling provides a means of preparing students to succeed on standardized and state assessments. Thirty copying masters and two practice tests offer students practice in reading, vocabulary, and spelling skills, while helping them become familiar with a variety of national and state test formats. *Practice for Assessment* includes the following.

Reading Masters   The reading masters provide reading support for the chapter-opener selections at the beginning of each composition chapter in the Pupil's Edition. The five reading questions, both multiple-choice and open-ended, give students the opportunity to practice a range of important reading skills, such as previewing, identifying the main idea and supporting details, interpreting figurative language, and making inferences.

Vocabulary Masters   Each vocabulary master introduces ten vocabulary words taken from the vocabulary list that appears in *Academic and Workplace Skills,* pages 51–52. In the five practice exercises that make up each master, students are given the opportunity to use these words in a variety of contexts. The exercises on the vocabulary masters help students develop critical acquisition and retention skills, such as using context clues and analyzing word parts.

Spelling Masters   Each spelling master introduces ten new spelling words taken from the *Elements of Writing* spelling list (Pupil's Edition, pages 791–793). Five short practice exercises offer students numerous ways to learn the new words by focusing on skills proven to increase spelling ability, such as recognizing sound-symbol relationships, identifying letter patterns, spelling words with affixes, and proofreading.

Practice Tests   Two practice tests, each containing twenty-five items that reflect the various test formats students will encounter on standardized tests, give students practice in test taking and allow you to assess the skills that are addressed on the reading, vocabulary, and spelling masters.

Teaching Notes and Answer Keys   Teaching notes and answer keys are provided for all of the worksheets. The teaching notes provide instructional objectives, teaching suggestions, and extension activities. The answer keys are included at the back of the booklet.

You can use the copying masters in a variety of ways. For example, you can assign students a master to complete in one sitting, or you can use one master over the course of a week, assigning one exercise as a quick warm-up and focus activity at the beginning of each class period. In response to many teachers' concerns about limited time and resources, these masters have been designed so they can be copied on transparencies to use with the entire class, or copied as class sets that can be reused.

Practice for Assessment is eighth in a series of eight booklets comprising the **Teaching Resources.**

- *Practicing the Writing Process*
- *Strategies for Writing*
- *Word Choice and Sentence Style*
- *Language Skills Practice and Assessment*
- *Academic and Workplace Skills*
- *Holistic Scoring: Prompts and Models*
- *Portfolio Assessment*
- **Practice for Assessment in Reading, Vocabulary, and Spelling**

Reading Master 1

▶ This master is designed to be used with the excerpt from "Questions and Answers" by Dudley Randall on pages 20–22 in your textbook. Using your own paper, answer the following questions based on the selection.

1. *Demonstrating Comprehension* According to Dudley Randall, what should beginning poets do before they consider sending their poems to various publications?

2. *Identifying Supporting Details* Which of the following statements does *not* support Randall's ideas on young poets and their poetry?

A. Young poets are exploring new forms and ideas.

B. Young poets should gain a good knowledge of spelling and grammar.

C. Young poets are unsophisticated and write poorly.

D. Young poets should publish their poems in periodicals, not in books.

3. *Identifying Problem-Solution Relationships* To eliminate overused expressions from one's writing, Randall recommends

A. keeping a poem private and not allowing it to be read

B. reading widely to recognize expressions that have lost their freshness

C. trying to use fresher clichés that have been only slightly overused

D. asking a teacher to read and criticize one's work

4. *Identifying the Author's Viewpoint* Which of the following statements does *not* represent Randall's thoughts on publishing poetry?

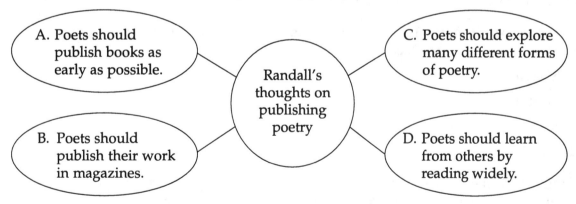

A. Poets should publish books as early as possible.

B. Poets should publish their work in magazines.

Randall's thoughts on publishing poetry

C. Poets should explore many different forms of poetry.

D. Poets should learn from others by reading widely.

5. *Evaluating Source Credibility and Reliability* Which response *best* explains why beginning poets might find Randall's opinions credible?

A. Randall knows the work of poet Robert Hayden.

B. Randall has studied the poems of Mari Evans.

C. Randall can recognize clichés and overused expressions.

D. Randall has edited and published the work of many poets.

Reading Master 2

▶ This master is designed to be used with the excerpt from *Black Elk Speaks* as told through John G. Neihardt on pages 60–62 in your textbook. Using your own paper, answer the following questions based on the selection.

1. ***Demonstrating Comprehension***   What events does Black Elk describe?

2. ***Skimming and Scanning***   Black Elk is told that a black wagon pulled by two black horses carries

   A. Victoria, the queen of England

   B. Grandmother England's grandson

   C. relatives of Queen Victoria

   D. soldiers and Wasichus

3. ***Identifying Sequence of Events***   The boxes below show some of the events described in the selection. Which of the statements that follow belongs in box 3?

The Wild West Show goes to perform for Queen Victoria.	Queen Victoria rides around the show place.		Black Elk's people sing a song for Queen Victoria.
1	2	3	4

   A. The Wasichus murder Crazy Horse.

   B. The women make a tremolo.

   C. The Wasichus shout "Jubilee! Jubilee!"

   D. Queen Victoria shakes hands with Black Elk's people.

4. ***Identifying the Author's Tone***   Which of the following adjectives *best* describes Black Elk's attitude toward Queen Victoria?

   A. indifferent

   B. respectful

   C. envious

   D. distrustful

5. ***Making Inferences***   From the final sentence in the selection, readers can infer that Black Elk believes that under the leadership of Queen Victoria his people

   A. might have been exploited less and respected more

   B. would have had shining wagons and fine horses

   C. would not have participated in the jubilee

   D. might have suffered even greater hardships

Reading Master 3

▶ This master is designed to be used with "The Spaceport Mermaids" by Greg Walz-Chojnacki on pages 94–95 in your textbook. Using your own paper, answer the following questions based on the selection.

1. *Previewing* Before you read, take a look at the title, illustrations, and captions that accompany the selection. Based on what you see, what do you think the selection will be about?

2. *Demonstrating Comprehension* According to the article, why are manatees associated with mermaids?

A. Historic literature often pairs manatees and mermaids.

B. At sea, swimming mermaids resemble swimming manatees.

C. Both mermaids and manatees are imaginary creatures.

D. Superstitious seamen may have mistaken manatees for mermaids.

3. *Identifying Cause-and-Effect Relationships* Complete the chart below by choosing the statement that *best* completes the cause-and-effect relationship described in the selection.

Cause		Effect
NASA has protected manatees since 1977.	→	

A. Some manatees wear radio monitors.

B. Manatees are often injured by the propellers of power boats.

C. The number of manatees at the space center has increased.

D. Manatee deaths have increased in Florida.

4. *Making Inferences* From the description of the boats NASA uses to retrieve solid rocket boosters, readers can infer that

A. water jets are more powerful than propellers

B. water jets are less harmful to manatees than propellers

C. manatees use water jets to protect themselves from boats

D. NASA employees prefer to use boats with propellers

5. *Identifying the Main Idea* Which of the following statements *best* summarizes the main idea of the selection?

A. The number of manatee deaths is growing in Florida.

B. People should not use propeller-driven power boats.

C. NASA should be allowed to protect more endangered species.

D. Manatees thrive in the waters of the Kennedy Space Center.

Reading Master 4

▶ This master is designed to be used with "The Jacket" by Gary Soto on pages 116–121 in your textbook. Using your own paper, answer the following questions based on the selection.

1. **Demonstrating Comprehension** What reasons does the boy give for not liking the jacket?

2. **Identifying Sequence of Events** The boxes below show some things that happened in the story. Which of the statements that follow belongs in box 4?

The boy gets a new jacket that he thinks is very ugly.	The boy wears the ugly jacket for a long time.	The jacket begins to crack and lose its stuffing.	
1	2	3	4

   A. The boy throws the ugly jacket in the garbage.

   B. The boy's mother makes him keep the jacket.

   C. The boy buys a new, better-looking jacket.

   D. The mother sends the jacket to a child in Mexico.

3. **Identifying Figurative Language** Which of the following lines from the selection includes an example of personification?

   A. "I . . . approached the jacket slowly, as if it were a stranger whose hand I had to shake."

   B. "From the kitchen mother yelled that my jacket was in the closet."

   C. "I got up . . . and went to my bedroom to sit with my jacket on my lap . . ."

   D. "That winter the elbows began to crack and whole chunks of green began to fall off."

4. **Making Inferences** From the last sentence in the selection, readers can infer that

   A. the boy wears the jacket for the rest of his life

   B. the boy finally gives the jacket to his younger brother

   C. the jacket remains an important but negative figure in the boy's life

   D. the boy realizes he loves the jacket even though it is ugly

5. **Identifying the Main Idea** Which of the following sentences *best* expresses the main idea of the selection?

   A. The boy should not be forced to wear an ugly jacket to school.

   B. The boy believes the jacket caused some bad experiences in fifth and sixth grades.

   C. Even though the boy doesn't like the jacket, it always keeps him warm.

   D. The boy's mother does not understand how important fashion is to a teenager.

Reading Master 5

▶ This master is designed to be used with the excerpt from *Nisei Daughter* by Monica Sone on pages 150–151 in your textbook. Using your own paper, answer the following questions based on the selection.

1. Demonstrating Comprehension   According to the selection, *osushi* is

A. raw fish

B. bean soup

C. rice cakes with seaweed

D. puffed-up marshmallows

2. Identifying Sensory Language   Copy the following chart onto your paper. For each of the categories listed in the chart, identify at least one example of sensory language from the selection.

Sensory Category	Example of Sensory Language
Visual Details	
Sounds	
Tastes	
Smells	

3. Interpreting Figurative Language   Why does Sone compare *mochi* to "oversized marshmallows" and *kimpira* to "a mass of brown twigs"?

A. to help readers imagine how these foods look

B. to help readers imagine how these foods taste

C. to describe the sweet bean soup

D. to describe the spicy burdock

4. Identifying the Author's Purpose   The author most likely wrote this passage in order to

A. persuade readers to try Japanese food

B. explain how to prepare several Japanese dishes

C. describe a memorable Japanese meal

D. discuss the strengths and weaknesses of Japanese cooking

5. Identifying the Author's Tone   Which of the following words *best* describes the author's tone in the passage?

A. disinterested

B. nostalgic

C. critical

D. sad

Reading Master 6

▶ This master is designed to be used with "Coyote Places the Stars" by Barry Lopez on pages 180–182 in your textbook. Using your own paper, answer the following questions based on the selection.

1. ***Making Predictions*** Based on the illustration and the title of the selection, predict what the selection will be about.

2. ***Demonstrating Comprehension*** Coyote's trick

   A. creates a star formation called Big Dipper

   B. leaves the five wolves stranded and starving

   C. leads to the death of two grizzly bears

   D. was made possible by the wolf's dog

3. ***Skimming and Scanning*** How many animals climb the arrow ladder?

   A. nine

   B. six

   C. eight

   D. seven

4. ***Identifying Sequence of Events*** The boxes below show some things that happened in the story. Which of the statements that follow belongs in box 2?

Coyote and the wolves see two animals in the sky.		Coyote and the wolves climb up the ladder into the sky.	Coyote leaves the wolves sitting with the bears.
1	2	3	4

   A. Coyote tells Meadowlark about the stars.

   B. Coyote tells the wolves the animals are bears.

   C. The wolves share their food with Coyote.

   D. Coyote makes a ladder out of arrows.

5. ***Drawing Conclusions*** Based on Coyote's words and actions, readers can conclude that the reason Coyote abandons the animals in the sky is that

   A. he enjoys playing practical jokes on his friends

   B. he wishes to get revenge on the animals

   C. he wants to gain fame and be remembered

   D. he likes to show off his supernatural powers

Reading Master 7

▶ This master is designed to be used with "How to Eat Like a Child" by Delia Ephron on pages 212–214 in your textbook. Using your own paper, answer the following questions based on the selection.

1. **Activating Prior Knowledge**   Choose a food such as an ice-cream cone or corn on the cob. Before you read the selection, write down some basic instructions on how to eat that food.

2. **Demonstrating Comprehension**   The writer gives directions on how to eat all of the following foods except

   A. peas

   B. pizza

   C. spaghetti

   D. french fries

3. **Skimming and Scanning**   Skim the selection to identify the alternative method the author recommends for eating mashed potatoes.

   A. Mash flat and create gravy ponds.

   B. Mix with ketchup until pink.

   C. Flatten with the back of a fork.

   D. Divide into piles and then rearrange.

4. **Outlining**   The outline below is based on information from the selection. From the choices in the right-hand column, choose the *best* entry to fill in the blank.

   How to Eat Like a Child

   I. Eating Spaghetti
      A. Eat noisily
      B. Spill leftovers

   II. Eating an Ice-Cream Cone
      A. Knock off top scoop
      B. _____

   III. Eating Chocolate-Chip Cookies
      A. Get crumbs in bed
      B. Eat chips separately

   A. Eating Cooked Carrots

   B. Divide into little piles

   C. Leave on car dashboard

   D. Eating Ice Cream in a Bowl

5. **Making Inferences**   From the tone of the selection, readers can infer that the writer is

   A. seriously attempting to teach children the best ways to eat certain foods

   B. humorously describing how children eat certain foods

   C. poking fun at the ways some children show others how to eat certain foods

   D. encouraging children to change the ways they eat certain foods

Reading Master 8

▶ This master is designed to be used with the advertisement on page 244 in your textbook. Using your own paper, answer the following questions based on the selection.

1. **Previewing**   Before you read, take a look at the large print and illustrations that make up the selection. Based on what you see, what do you guess is being advertised?

2. **Demonstrating Comprehension**   The advertisement is promoting the consumption of

   A. fruits and vegetables

   B. dairy products

   C. milk and cereal

   D. alternatives to vitamins

3. **Identifying the Author's Purpose**   This advertisement was most likely designed to

   A. explore the benefits and dangers of dairy foods

   B. compare and contrast milk and bananas

   C. persuade readers to buy dairy foods

   D. inform readers about various dairy foods

4. **Drawing Conclusions**   Which of the following items is *not* a conclusion readers can make about dairy foods based on the information presented in the ad?

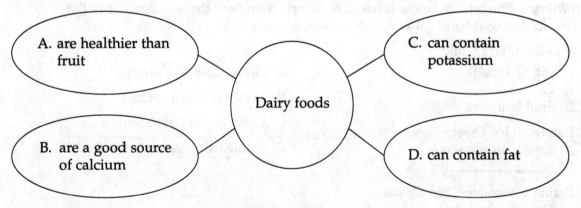

A. are healthier than fruit

B. are a good source of calcium

Dairy foods

C. can contain potassium

D. can contain fat

5. **Identifying Persuasive Techniques**   This advertisement attempts to persuade readers to buy dairy foods by

   A. presenting facts about the nutritional benefits of dairy foods

   B. using a celebrity to tell about the benefits of dairy foods

   C. attacking fruits as an inadequate source of nutrition

   D. using a short, catchy phrase that readers will remember

Reading Master 9

▶ This master is designed to be used with the review of Lois Lowry's *Number the Stars* by Louise L. Sherman on pages 276–277 in your textbook. Using your own paper, answer the following questions based on the selection.

1. **Demonstrating Comprehension**   Copy the following T-chart onto your paper. Complete the chart by listing in the appropriate column the reviewer's descriptions of Annemarie as a child and as a Resistance worker.

Annemarie as a child	Annemarie as a Resistance worker

2. **Identifying the Main Idea**   Which of the following statements *best* describes the author's overall opinion of *Number the Stars*?

   A. The book focuses too much on the Resistance effort.

   B. The character Annemarie is brave and inspiring.

   C. The topic is not appropriate for children's books.

   D. The book is inspirational and appropriate for children.

3. **Drawing Conclusions**   From the author's description of the Danish people's effective actions during World War II, readers can conclude that

   A. many young people protested Nazi persecution

   B. many Jews were able to escape to other countries

   C. the Danish Resistance was conducted especially well

   D. ship captains smuggled Jews to many other countries

4. **Identifying the Author's Tone**   When the author says the book "reiterates the inspirational idealism of the young people," she is

   A. criticizing the young people for their idealism

   B. questioning the significance of their efforts in the Resistance

   C. praising the adults for inspiring the Danish youth

   D. showing her admiration for the young people in the Resistance

5. **Distinguishing Fact from Opinion**   Which of the following quotations from the review is a statement of fact?

   A. "Annemarie is not just a symbol . . ."

   B. "An afterword answers the questions that readers will have . . ."

   C. "She is a very real child . . ."

   D. "It is well plotted, and period and place are convincingly recreated."

Reading Master 10

▶ This master is designed to be used with the excerpt from *Meet-a-Cheetah* by Fred Johnson on pages 316–317 in your textbook. Using your own paper, answer the following questions based on the selection.

1. Demonstrating Comprehension   According to the selection, how fast can a cheetah run?

A. up to 60 miles an hour

B. up to 70 miles an hour

C. up to 80 miles an hour

D. up to 100 miles an hour

2. Identifying Comparison and Contrast Relationships   Copy and complete the following chart. List information about cheetahs in the first column. Then, for each item in the "Cheetahs" column, place a check mark in one of the next two columns to show whether the cheetah shares each characteristic with cats or dogs.

Cheetahs	Cats	Dogs

3. Distinguishing Fact from Opinion   Which of the following statements from the selection is an opinion?

A. "Cheetahs are found in Africa, in India, Afghanistan, and Arabia."

B. "But like all cats, cheetahs have one claw that is very sharp and dangerous."

C. "The cheetah's sense of smell is poor, but its eyesight is keen."

D. "But the most amazing thing about cheetahs is their speed."

4. Identifying Supporting Details   The writer tells the story about the cheetah chasing the motorcycle to support the idea that

A. cheetahs are curious

B. cheetahs are very fast

C. cheetahs can be tamed

D. cheetahs can outrun anything

5. Summarizing   Which of the following statements *best* summarizes the selection's main idea?

A. Cheetahs are an endangered species that should be protected.

B. The cheetah's speed makes it dangerous.

C. The cheetah is more like a dog than like a cat.

D. Cheetahs are interesting, unique members of the cat family.

Vocabulary Master 1

adopt *vt.* to take up and use as one's own **anguish** *n.* great suffering or distress **exclude** *vt.* to refuse to admit or include; reject **infrequent** *adj.* happening seldom; rare **prudent** *adj.* cautious or discreet in conduct **recommend** *vt.* to suggest favorably	**subtle** *adj.* so slight as to be difficult to detect; not obvious **supervise** *vt.* to direct or manage **tactics** *n.* skillful methods or procedures used to achieve a goal **turmoil** *n.* a great disturbance or commotion

▶ Use your own paper to complete the following vocabulary exercises.

Exercise A: Collecting New Words Write the vocabulary words and their definitions in your vocabulary notebook.

Exercise B: Analyzing Word Parts In a chart like the one below, identify and define the roots and affixes in the vocabulary words *exclude, infrequent,* and *supervise*. Then explain how the affixes affect the meanings of the roots to result in the vocabulary words.

Vocabulary Word	Affix(es)	Root	Effect on Meaning
recommend	prefix *re–*, "again, over again"	*–commend–* "to express approval or praise"	Adding the prefix to the root creates a verb meaning "to express approval or praise again."

Exercise C: Using Context Clues Use context clues to help determine which vocabulary words *best* complete the paragraph below.

Carla was moved as she witnessed the __1__ of the family whose home was destroyed in the fire. She thought about her own family's rare discussions of fire safety and wished they were not so __2__ . It would be wise to __3__ the habit of practicing how to exit the house in case of a fire.

Exercise D: Using Real-Life Vocabulary Your sports team is preparing for an important game, and your coach has asked for ideas on how to defeat your rivals. Use the following vocabulary words in a brief report describing your ideas.

adopt	prudent	tactics	recommend	supervise

Exercise E: Selecting Synonyms For each sentence below, decide which of the four choices has most nearly the *same* meaning as the word in italics.

1. The dress had a *subtle* design of white flowers on a white background.
   A. gorgeous
   B. idle
   C. elegant
   D. delicate

2. The village was in *turmoil* as people tried to flee before the volcano erupted.
   A. reaction
   B. confusion
   C. discomfort
   D. calm

Vocabulary Master 2

aerial *adj.* of, in, or by the air **destiny** *n.* inevitable order of events; fate **edible** *adj.* fit to be eaten **eloquent** *adj.* characterized by graceful, vivid, and persuasive communication **motive** *n.* a desire or impulse that leads to action	**offend** *vt.* to cause someone to feel angry, resentful, or hurt **repel** *vt.* to drive or force back **timid** *adj.* easily frightened; shy **tutor** *n.* a private teacher **versatile** *adj.* able or skilled in many things

▶ Use your own paper to complete the following vocabulary exercises.

Exercise A: Collecting New Words   Write the vocabulary words and their definitions in your vocabulary notebook.

Exercise B: Analyzing Word Origins and Etymologies   Write the vocabulary word that matches each etymology below. Then explain how the origin and modern meaning of each word are related.

1. From the Latin word *edere*, "eat," and the Latin suffix *–ibilis*, "able"

2. From the Latin prefix *e–*, "out," the Latin word *loqui*, "to speak," and the Latin suffix *–entis*, "that does"

3. From the Latin prefix *ob–*, "against," and the Latin word *fendere*, "to strike"

Exercise C: Demonstrating Understanding   Answer each question below, and explain your response. Your explanation should clearly show that you understand the meaning of the word in italics.

1. Where might you see an *aerial* acrobatic display?

2. Do you believe in *destiny*?

3. What are some likely *motives* for wanting to do well in school?

4. How would a *timid* person react in a room full of strangers?

Exercise D: Recognizing Denotation   For each pair of sentences below, use definition and context to choose the sentence that uses the vocabulary word correctly.

1.	A. The offensive line *repelled* the players who were rushing the quarterback.	B. The small boat was *repelled* by an outboard motor and could be maneuvered easily.
2.	A. She was a *versatile* swimmer, so she won many races in her specialty.	B. The *versatile* actor played in comedies as well as dramas and musicals.

Exercise E: Selecting Synonyms   For each phrase below, decide which of the four choices has most nearly the *same* meaning as the italicized word.

1. An *eloquent* speaker
   A. ambitious
   B. genuine
   C. expressive
   D. severe

2. A private *tutor*
   A. player
   B. instructor
   C. coach
   D. specialist

Vocabulary Master 3

abstract *adj.* not material; not concrete	**gratify** *vt.* to give pleasure or satisfaction to
caliber *n.* the worth or quality of something	**impact** *n.* a collision; the force of a collision
conform *vi.* to be or become similar	**incredible** *adj.* unbelievable; seemingly impossible
elaborate *adj.* intricate; rich in detail	**manual** *n.* a book of instructions; a handbook
grammatical *adj.* of or relating to grammar	**modest** *adj.* not vain or boastful; unassuming

▶ Use your own paper to complete the following vocabulary exercises.

Exercise A: Collecting New Words Write the vocabulary words and their definitions in your vocabulary notebook.

Exercise B: Determining Meanings of Words with Greek and Latin Roots
Study the information below, and explain in your own words how the parts of each vocabulary word combine to create its meaning.

Vocabulary Word	Prefix	Root	Suffix
1. conform	*con–*, "together"	L. *–form–*, "form"	
2. grammatical		L. *–gramma–*, "something written"	L. *–atic*, "of, of the kind of" + *–al*, "of, like"
3. gratify		L. *–grat–*, "please, favor"	L. *–fy*, "to cause to feel"

Exercise C: Determining the Meanings of Multiple-Meaning Words Many of the vocabulary words above have more than one meaning. Study how the vocabulary words are used in the sentences below, determine their parts of speech, and write a short definition for each word.

1. Mike enjoys working with his hands; he doesn't mind *manual* work at all.

2. Paul makes sure his motocross bike *conforms* to the rules of the racing committee.

3. The economic *impact* of the Depression lasted until the Second World War.

4. The Ramirezes bought a *modest* home rather than a large, showy mansion.

Exercise D: Relating Dictionary Definitions to Context Identify the appropriate definition according to how the vocabulary words *abstract* and *caliber* are used in each context below.

1. Rafael enjoyed his English and science classes more than algebra, which he found difficult and *abstract*.	**abstract** *adj.* **1** separate from material objects **2** hard to understand
2. The high *caliber* of her woodworking skills meant that Madeline's creations were always in demand.	**caliber** *n.* **1** the quality of a person or thing **2** the size of a bullet or shell **3** the diameter of the bore of a gun

Exercise E: Selecting Antonyms For each item below, decide which of the four choices has most nearly the *opposite* meaning of the word given.

1. incredible
   A. inedible
   B. doubtful
   C. believable
   D. ordinary

2. elaborate
   A. inexpensive
   B. adorned
   C. unattractive
   D. simple

Vocabulary Master 4

aggravate *vt.* to make worse or more unpleasant	**ignorance** *n.* lack of knowledge
commit *vt.* to bind as with a promise; pledge	**irritable** *adj.* easily annoyed or provoked
comparable *adj.* alike enough to be compared	**recognition** *n.* awareness of someone or something as having been known before
confirm *vt.* to prove to be true	
distort *vt.* to alter from the usual shape	**veto** *n.* an order preventing some proposed act
excess *n.* an amount greater than necessary	

▶ Use your own paper to complete the following vocabulary exercises.

Exercise A: Collecting New Words   Write the vocabulary words and their definitions in your vocabulary notebook.

Exercise B: Analyzing Word Origins and Etymologies   Use a dictionary to research the origin of each vocabulary word below. Then explain how the origin and modern meaning of each word are related.

1. veto   2. aggravate   3. distort   4. recognition

Exercise C: Using Context Clues   Use context clues to help determine which vocabulary words *best* complete the paragraph below.

Last year I fell off my bike one day on my way home from school. I knew right away something was wrong because my leg hurt pretty badly, and I couldn't walk at all. When we got to the hospital, it only took the doctor about five minutes to __1__ that my leg was broken. I had to stay home for weeks. I got pretty grouchy and __2__ because I had nothing to do. My little brother wasn't very helpful. He __3__ the situation by constantly teasing me about my accident.

Exercise D: Using Word Families   Copy and complete the following chart by listing other words in the same word families.

Noun	Verb	Adjective
1	commit	committable
2	3	comparable
ignorance	4	5

Exercise E: Selecting Synonyms   For each sentence below, decide which of the four choices has most nearly the *same* meaning as the word in italics.

1. Sandy applied the wood stain evenly with a cloth and then wiped off the *excess*.
   A. recess
   B. extra
   C. quantity
   D. supply

2. Even though one suit was much less expensive than the other, they were of *comparable* quality.
   A. similar
   B. average
   C. distinct
   D. different

Vocabulary Master 5

camouflage *n.* a disguise that allows a person or thing to blend with the surroundings **effect** *n.* any result brought about by a cause **loiter** *vi.* to walk or move slowly, with frequent stops **merit** *vt.* to deserve or be worthy of **myth** *n.* a traditional story used to explain human nature, a natural phenomenon, etc.	**notable** *adj.* worthy of notice; remarkable **ridicule** *vt.* to make the object of scornful laughter; to make fun of **satellite** *n.* a moon or artificial object that orbits a planet **tranquil** *adj.* free from disturbance; calm **vague** *adj.* not sharp, certain, or precise; unclear

▶ Use your own paper to complete the following vocabulary exercises.

Exercise A: Collecting New Words   Write the vocabulary words and their definitions in your vocabulary notebook.

Exercise B: Recognizing Words from Other Languages   The following English words were borrowed or adapted from other languages. Use a dictionary to research each word's origins, and explain how its original meaning is connected with its meaning in English.

   1. loiter   2. myth   3. satellite   4. camouflage

Exercise C: Recognizing Connotation   Read the sentences below, and describe the connotations you associate with each word in italics.

1. Marta had been *ridiculed* about her height at school and was always sensitive about it afterward.

2. One of the attractions of fishing is spending time in a boat on a quiet, *tranquil* lake.

3. Some people believe that the moon is made of cheese, but I know that's a *myth*.

4. Business owners sometimes object when people *loiter* in their stores.

Exercise D: Using Real-Life Vocabulary   A good friend is being considered for recognition at a school awards ceremony. Use the following vocabulary words in a letter of recommendation telling why your friend deserves an award.

effect	merit	loiter	notable	vague

Exercise E: Selecting Synonyms   For each phrase below, decide which of the four choices has most nearly the *same* meaning as the word in italics.

1. A *tranquil* outlook
  A. joyous
  B. serene
  C. silent
  D. hectic
	2. A *vague* plan
	  A. imprudent
	  B. indefinite
	  C. mysterious
	  D. accurate

Vocabulary Master 6

dual *adj.* consisting of two parts or kinds	**manuscript** *n.* a handwritten or typed version of a document
geological *adj.* of or about the study of the earth	**phase** *n.* a stage of development
hostile *adj.* showing ill will; unfriendly	**propel** *vt.* to push or drive forward
intermediate *adj.* in the middle	**stationary** *adj.* not moving; fixed
kernel *n.* the central or most important part of something	**submerged** *adj.* under or covered with liquid

▶ Use your own paper to complete the following vocabulary exercises.

Exercise A: Collecting New Words Write the vocabulary words and their definitions in your vocabulary notebook.

Exercise B: Determining Meanings of Words with Greek and Latin Roots
Study the information below, and explain in your own words how the parts of each vocabulary word combine to create its meaning.

Vocabulary Word	Prefix	Root	Suffix
1. manuscript	L. *manu–*, "hand"	L. *–script–*, "write"	
2. geological	Gr. *geo–*, "earth"	Gr. *–logy–*, "science"	*–ical*, "having to do with"
3. submerged	L. *sub–*, "under"	L. *–merg–*, "plunge"	*–ed* (here, indicates adj.)

Exercise C: Determining the Meanings of Homonyms Use context clues to help determine which word in parentheses *best* completes each sentence below.

1. Riding a *(stationary, stationery)* bicycle is an effective way to exercise at home.

2. Since each swordsman claimed to be the greatest, a *(dual, duel)* was inevitable.

3. Reading over her first draft, Phyllis decided that she would rewrite much of her report but would keep the *(kernel, colonel)* of her thesis.

4. With two outs and the score tied, the pressure was on. However, the tense situation didn't seem to *(phase, faze)* Rodney at all.

Exercise D: Demonstrating Understanding Answer each question below, and explain your response. Your explanation should clearly show that you understand the meaning of the word in italics.

1. What *propels* a vacuum cleaner? a toy car?

2. Why might two people who had been close become *hostile* toward each other?

3. What things are often *submerged*? Name two.

4. If you took Spanish, would you be in an *intermediate* class?

Exercise E: Selecting Antonyms For each item below, decide which of the four choices has most nearly the *opposite* meaning of the word given.

1. stationary
   A. firm
   B. immobile
   C. dashing
   D. movable

2. propel
   A. retreat
   B. retire
   C. repel
   D. reroute

Vocabulary Master 7

banish *vt.* to exile; to get rid of; to force to leave	**overture** *n.* an act or proposal that shows willing-ness to negotiate
flaw *n.* an imperfection; a defect	
habitat *n.* the place where an animal or plant natu-rally lives or grows	**radiate** *vt.* to send out rays of light or heat; to give forth or spread
immune *adj.* protected from something harmful	**refrain** *vi.* to hold back; to keep oneself from doing something
magnitude *n.* greatness in size, scope, or influence	
obsolete *adj.* no longer used or done; out-of-date	**speculate** *vi.* to think about or consider; to guess

▶ Use your own paper to complete the following vocabulary exercises.

Exercise A: Collecting New Words   Write the vocabulary words and their defini-tions in your vocabulary notebook.

Exercise B: Identifying Technical and Specialized Terms   In addition to the definitions given above, each of the following words also has a particular meaning in a specific field. Use your dictionary to research these special meanings. Write the special definition of each word, along with a sentence that shows your understanding of this definition.

    1. refrain (music)   2. magnitude (astronomy)   3. overture (music)

Exercise C: Using Real-Life Vocabulary   Hunting animals for food is an issue on which there are a variety of viewpoints. Use the following words in a letter to the editor in which you discuss the views of hunters or of those opposed to hunting.

speculate	habitat	refrain	obsolete	magnitude

Exercise D: Recognizing Denotation   For each pair of sentences below, use definition and context to choose the sentence that uses the vocabulary word correctly.

1.	A. The *flaw* that Marissa found in the pottery made her reconsider buying it for her mother.	B. Marissa felt that her recital perform-ance was her best ever, it was so passionate and full of *flaws*.
2.	A. The old heater could still *radiate* enough heat to make the room cozy.	B. The technician *radiated* Joe's arm to take an X-ray of the break.

Exercise E: Selecting Synonyms   For each sentence below, decide which of the four choices has most nearly the *same* meaning as the word in italics.

    1. Because of his disobedience, Sir Ethelred was *banished* from the kingdom.
        A. exclaimed   C. expelled
        B. exported   D. exposed

    2. Because I have had chickenpox before, I am now *immune* to the disease.
        A. grateful   C. opposed
        B. resistant   D. adjacent

Vocabulary Master 8

abrupt *adj*. sudden and unexpected	**illustrious** *adj*. distinguished; outstanding
capacity *n*. the maximum amount something can hold	**indispensable** *adj*. absolutely essential; necessary
endurance *n*. the ability to withstand pain, fatigue, distress, hardship, etc.	**maternal** *adj*. of or like a mother; motherly
	pivot *vt*. to turn on or around
hysterical *adj*. having uncontrolled emotion	**prestige** *n*. the power to impress or influence
	revise *vt*. to change, correct, or improve

▶ Use your own paper to complete the following vocabulary exercises.

Exercise A: Collecting New Words   Write the vocabulary words and their definitions in your vocabulary notebook.

Exercise B: Analyzing Word Parts   In a chart like the one below, identify and define the roots and affixes in the vocabulary words *maternal, revise,* and *indispensable*. Then explain how the affixes affect the meanings of the roots to result in the vocabulary words.

Vocabulary Word	Affix(es)	Root	Effect on Meaning
endurance	prefix *en–*, "to make or make like"; suffix *–ance*, "the quality or state of being"	L.–*dur*– "hard"	Adding *en*– to the root forms the verb *endure*. The suffix *–ance* forms a noun meaning "the ability to withstand pain."

Exercise C: Recognizing Connotation   Read the sentences below, and describe the connotations you associate with each italicized word.

1. The Johnsons' reaction to winning the grand prize can be described as *hysterical*.

2. Accepting the award, Mona saw the *maternal* love and pride on her mother's face.

3. For Peter, an important reason for running for class president was the *prestige* he would have among his classmates.

Exercise D: Using Context Clues   Use context clues to help determine which vocabulary words *best* complete the paragraph below.

   The stadium was filled to __1__ , with five thousand people cheering the soccer teams competing for the division title. On the field, Rocky felt that all eyes were on him because he was __2__ , one of the team's best players. His teammate passed the ball to him, and Rocky jumped and __3__ in the air to head the ball into the opposing goal. The last few seconds of the match ticked away, and the stands exploded with the emotion of the spectators' __4__ celebration. Having scored the only goal in the match, Rocky was certainly the most distinguished and __5__ player on the field that day.

Exercise E: Selecting Synonyms   For each phrase below, decide which of the four choices has most nearly the *same* meaning as the word in italics.

1. an *abrupt* departure
   A. hasty
   B. prompt
   C. overdue
   D. expected

2. remarkable *endurance*
   A. ability
   B. pain
   C. tolerance
   D. speed

Vocabulary Master 9

audible *adj.* capable of being heard **avert** *vt.* to keep from happening; prevent **blemish** *n.* a mark, flaw, or defect that harms the appearance **diverse** *adj.* different; unlike; varied **expand** *vt.* to increase in size; to enlarge **fascinate** *vt.* to hold attention by being interesting	**inferior** *adj.* lower in importance, rank, order, or status **invade** *vt.* to enter by force; to intrude upon **patron** *n.* one who sponsors or supports a person, group, institution, etc. **vital** *adj.* essential; indispensable

▶ Use your own paper to complete the following vocabulary exercises.

Exercise A: Collecting New Words   Write the vocabulary words and their definitions in your vocabulary notebook.

Exercise B: Analyzing Word Origins and Etymologies   Use a dictionary to research the origin of each vocabulary word below. Then explain how the origin and modern meaning of each word are related.

1. vital   2. avert   3. patron   4. inferior

Exercise C: Using Word Families   Copy and complete the following chart by listing other words in the same word families.

Noun	Verb	Adjective
1	fascinate	2
3	invade	invasive
4	expand	5

Exercise D: Demonstrating Understanding   Answer each question below, and explain your response. Your explanation should clearly show that you understand the meaning of the italicized vocabulary word.

1. Would you be concerned if you discovered a *blemish* on your face before having your picture taken?

2. What sorts of *diverse* interests do you have?

3. What are three things you consider to be *vital* to a happy life?

4. Are there any noises you hear regularly that you wish were not *audible?*

Exercise E: Selecting Antonyms   For each item, decide which of the four choices has most nearly the *opposite* meaning of the word given.

1. An *inferior* product
   A. interior
   B. ulterior
   C. exterior
   D. superior

2. A *diverse* group of people
   A. tranquil
   B. comparable
   C. varied
   D. competent

Vocabulary Master 10

contemplate *vt.* to think about carefully	**pursue** *vt.* to chase; to follow
intolerable *adj.* unbearable; too much to be endured	**self-conscious** *adj.* awkward or embarrassed in the presence of others
legible *adj.* that can be read or deciphered	**undergrowth** *n.* low-growing plants of a forest
notorious *adj.* known widely but unfavorably	**velocity** *n.* rapidity of motion; speed; swiftness
precaution *n.* a measure taken in advance against possible harm or failure	**zoology** *n.* the branch of biology that deals with the study of animals

▶ Use your own paper to complete the following vocabulary exercises.

Exercise A: Collecting New Words   Write the vocabulary words and their definitions in your vocabulary notebook.

Exercise B: Determining Meanings of Words with Greek and Latin Roots
Study the information below, and explain in your own words how the parts of each vocabulary word combine to create its meaning.

Vocabulary Word	Prefix	Root	Suffix
1. zoology	Gr. *zo–*, "life, animal"	Gr. *–logy–*, "science"	
2. legible		L. *–leg–*, "read"	L. *–ible*, "able"
3. intolerable	L. *in–*, "not"	L. *–toler–*, "bear, sustain"	L. *–able*, "able"
4. velocity		L. *–velox–*, "swift, speedy"	L. *–ity*, "state or character"

Exercise C: Determining the Meanings of Compound Words   Identify the parts of each compound word below, and explain how they combine to form the word's meaning.

   1. undergrowth   2. self-conscious

Exercise D: Using Real-Life Vocabulary   Imagine that you're planning to write a mystery story. Answer the following questions about some of the details of your story.

   1. What *notorious* act will the villain commit?

   2. What *precautions* will the hero take to avoid being trapped by the villain?

   3. Where will the hero *pursue* the villain to put an end to the crimes?

Exercise E: Selecting Synonyms   For each sentence below, decide which of the four choices has most nearly the *same* meaning as the word in italics.

   1. Maria went to her room to *contemplate* the possibility of going to summer school.
     A. avert
     B. ponder
     C. dread
     D. resolve

   2. In the summer in Texas, the heat can become almost *intolerable*.
     A. inoffensive
     B. inaccessible
     C. unendurable
     D. undeniable

Spelling Master 1

acceptance	careless	existence	instead	ninety
again	committee	foreign	knowledge	villain

▶ Use your own paper to complete the following spelling exercises.

Exercise A: Collecting New Words   Copy the spelling words into your spelling notebook.

Exercise B: Recognizing Sound-Symbol Relationships   Identify and write the spelling words that contain the /e/ sound, as in *t*[e]*n*. Then draw a box around the /e/ sound in each word.

Exercise C: Dividing Words into Syllables   Divide the following spelling words into syllables by using slashes to mark the breaks.

   1. foreign   2. committee   3. villain   4. ninety

Exercise D: Spelling Words with Suffixes   Copy and complete the following chart. Fill in the spelling words that have the suffixes listed, and then write in the base word that combines with the suffix to form each spelling word. Finally, tell how the spelling of each base word changed when the suffix was added to it.

	Spelling Word	Base Word	Suffix
1.			–ance
2.			–ence
3.			–less
4.			–ty

Exercise E: Proofreading   For each group of sentences below, if one of the under-lined words is misspelled, write the letter for that sentence. If all the words are spelled correctly, write **D** for *No mistake.*

   1. A. I need to go to the library <u>again</u> to check out another book.
      B. There are no dinosaurs in <u>existance</u> today.
      C. To my <u>knowledge</u>, there is no meeting after school.
      D. No mistake

   2. A. My brother received his college <u>acceptance</u> letter yesterday.
      B. The <u>committee</u> decided to extend the park's hours during the summer.
      C. <u>Insted</u> of football, let's play another game more people know how to play.
      D. No mistake

Spelling Master 2

bicycle	country	favorite	sense	sympathy
bouquet	decision	genius	suspicion	treasury

▶ Use your own paper to complete the following spelling exercises.

Exercise A: Collecting New Words   Copy the spelling words into your spelling notebook.

Exercise B: Spelling Basic Sight Words   Identify and write the word that matches each phonetic spelling.

1. jēn′yəs	2. trezh′ər ē	3. fā′vər it	4. dē sizh′ən

Exercise C: Spelling Plurals   Write each of the following words in its plural form. Then explain what changes, if any, you had to make to the original word to make it plural.

1. bicycle   2. country   3. decision   4. genius   5. treasury

Exercise D: Analyzing Word Origins and Etymologies   Write the spelling word that matches each etymology below.

1. From the Latin prefix *bi–*, meaning "two," and the Greek word *kyklos*, meaning "a circle"

2. From the Old French word *bosquet*, meaning "a plume, nosegay"

3. From the Greek prefix *syn–*, meaning "together," and the Greek word *pathos*, meaning "feeling"

4. From the Latin word *suspicere*, meaning "to look secretly at, mistrust"

5. From the Latin word *sensus*, meaning "to feel, perceive"

Exercise E: Proofreading   For each sentence below, if one of the underlined words is misspelled, write the letter for that word. If all the words are spelled correctly, write **D** for *No mistake*.

1. My <u>favorite</u> book describes a character's <u>decision</u> to explore the world on his
   A   B
   <u>bycicle</u>. <u>No mistake</u>
   C   D

2. My <u>sense</u> of smell was awakened by the <u>boquet</u> of <u>country</u> flowers. <u>No mistake</u>
   A   B   C   D

3. The accounting <u>genious</u> found evidence to confirm our <u>suspicion</u> that someone was
   A   B
   taking money out of the club <u>treasury</u>. <u>No mistake</u>
   C   D

Spelling Master 3

accumulate	can't	doesn't	jealous	realize
argument	conscious	don't	nervous	won't

▶ Use your own paper to complete the following spelling exercises.

Exercise A: Collecting New Words   Copy the spelling words into your spelling notebook.

Exercise B: Recognizing Sound-Symbol Relationships   Identify and write the spelling words that contain the /ə/ sound, as in s⃞uspici⃞ou⃞s. Then draw a box around the /ə/ sound in each word.

Exercise C: Spelling Contractions   For each sentence below, write the correct contraction of each pair of words in parentheses.

1. I (can not) believe that they made a sequel to that movie!

2. My brother (does not) want to go to the arcade tonight.

3. The park ranger told us, "Please (do not) litter in the park."

4. The main menu (will not) return to the computer screen.

Exercise D: Spelling Words with Suffixes   Copy and complete the following chart. Choose a suffix to add to each spelling word listed, and write the new words you create. Then tell whether and how the spelling of each spelling word changed when the suffix was added to it.

	Spelling Word	Suffix	New Word	Change
Ex.	accumulate	–tion	accumulation	drop –e
1.	argument			
2.	conscious			
3.	jealous			
4.	nervous			
5.	realize			

Exercise E: Choosing Correct Spellings   For each sentence below, write the letter of the word that is spelled correctly and *best* completes the sentence.

1. The snow began to _____ on the frozen ground.
   A. acumulate
   B. acummulate
   C. accummulate
   D. accumulate

2. Luckily, I wasn't _____ when the dentist drilled into my tooth's nerve.
   A. conscience
   B. conscious
   C. consious
   D. conscous

Spelling Master 4

acquire	brief	criticize	interpret	speech
across	control	extremely	privilege	strength

▶ Use your own paper to complete the following spelling exercises.

Exercise A: Collecting New Words   Copy the spelling words into your spelling notebook.

Exercise B: Identifying Patterns   Identify and write the spelling words that contain one or more consonant combinations, as in *responsibility, machine,* and *campaign.* Then draw a box around the consonant combination(s) in each word.

Exercise C: Spelling Basic Sight Words   Identify and write the word that matches each phonetic spelling.

1. brēf   2. priv′ə lij   3. ə krôs′   4. krit′ə sīz′   5. ə kwīr′

Exercise D: Recognizing Word Shapes   Write the spelling word that matches each shape below.

1.
2.
3.
4.
5.

Exercise E: Proofreading   For each group of sentences below, if one of the under-lined words is misspelled, write the letter for that sentence. If all the words are spelled correctly, write **D** for *No mistake.*

1. A. Denise <u>criticized</u> her brother for keeping his room so messy.
   B. Everyone in this class will be treated the same—no special <u>priviledges</u>.
   C. My pen pal lives in Asia. That's halfway <u>across</u> the world!
   D. No mistake

2. A. Before you determine what type of career to pursue, you need to be aware of your <u>strenths</u> and weaknesses.
   B. Research shows that it can take up to seven years to <u>acquire</u> a new language completely.
   C. I have to give a <u>speech</u> today in social studies.
   D. No mistake

Spelling Master 5

apparent	candidate	efficiency	judgment	personal
audience	correspondence	fortunately	occasion	temperament

▶ Use your own paper to complete the following spelling exercises.

Exercise A: Collecting New Words   Copy the spelling words into your spelling notebook.

Exercise B: Identifying Patterns   Unscramble the letters below to write each spelling word correctly.

1. perapant

2. cosainoc

3. undaecie

4. mundgjet

5. metpetamern

Exercise C: Dividing Words into Syllables   Divide the following spelling words into syllables by using slashes to mark the breaks.

1. apparent   2. candidate   3. efficiency   4. judgment   5. occasion

Exercise D: Analyzing Word Origins and Etymologies   Write the spelling word that matches each etymology below.

1. From the Latin word *candidatus,* meaning "white-robed"

2. From the Latin word *persona,* meaning "actor's mask," and the Latin suffix *–al,* meaning "of, like, or suitable for"

3. From the Latin prefix *com–,* meaning "together," the Latin word *respondere,* meaning "to respond," and the Old French suffix *–ence,* meaning "act or quality"

4. From the Latin word *fortuna,* meaning "chance, fate," and the Old English suffix *–ly,* meaning "like, characteristic of"

5. From the Latin word *audientia,* meaning "a hearing, listening"

Exercise E: Proofreading   For each group of words below, if one of the words is misspelled, write the letter for that word. If all the words are spelled correctly, write **D** for *No mistake.*

1. A. personal
   B. eficiency
   C. apparent
   D. No mistake

2. A. occasion
   B. judgement
   C. audience
   D. No mistake

Spelling Master 6

bough	could	though	throughout	trouble
cough	straight	through	tonight	whose

▶ Use your own paper to complete the following spelling exercises.

Exercise A: Collecting New Words Copy the spelling words into your spelling notebook.

Exercise B: Recognizing Sound-Symbol Relationships Identify and write the spelling words that contain the consonant combination *gh*. Then draw a box around this letter grouping in each word.

Exercise C: Recognizing Word Shapes Write the spelling word that matches each shape below.

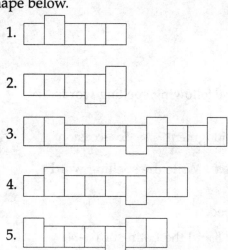

1.

2.

3.

4.

5.

Exercise D: Spelling Homonyms For each sentence below, identify and write the correct word from the pair in parentheses.

1. The strong winds caused the tree's (*bow, bough*) to break.

2. Kiri took a (*bow, bough*) at the end of her musical performance.

3. (*Whose, Who's*) supposed to take out the trash today?

4. Lizette, (*whose, who's*) dog ran away, is posting signs describing her lost pet.

5. Jacob accidentally (*threw, through*) the softball right (*threw, through*) the glass window.

Exercise E: Proofreading For each sentence below, if one of the underlined words is misspelled, write the letter for that word. If all the words are spelled correctly, write **D** for *No mistake*.

1. Because this <u>cough</u> <u>could</u> be contagious, I went <u>straight</u> to bed. <u>No mistake</u>
            A   B   C   D

2. Dakota, <u>who's</u> car was having <u>trouble</u>, missed the show <u>tonight</u>. <u>No mistake</u>
        A   B   C   D

Spelling Master 7

definite	execute	mischief	receive	university
describe	interest	perceive	transferred	unnecessary

▶ Use your own paper to complete the following spelling exercises.

Exercise A: Collecting New Words Copy the spelling words into your spelling notebook.

Exercise B: Recognizing Sound-Symbol Relationships Identify and write the spelling words that contain the /ē/ sound, as in *believe*. Then draw a box around the /ē/ sound in each word.

Exercise C: Identifying Missing Letters The following letter puzzles contain the vowels from certain spelling words. Identify and write each of the spelling words.

1. | | i | | | i | e | |
2. | | e | | | i | | e |
3. | i | | e | e | | |
4. | | e | i | i | | e |
5. | | e | | e | i | | e |

Exercise D: Proofreading The following paragraph contains five spelling errors. Identify and correctly write the words that are misspelled.

   The other day, my brother said he wanted to tell me an interesting story. He said that when my father was a student, he was transfered to a different universty because of some mischeif that he had executed. He started to describe the incident, but I told him that it was unneccesary. Our father had already told me the story. I could percieve my brother's disappointment. He had obviously wanted to surprise me.

Exercise E: Choosing Correct Spellings For each sentence below, write the letter of the word that is spelled correctly and *best* completes the sentence.

1. Students' _____ in the new after-school tutoring program is growing.
   A. intrest
   B. interest
   C. interst
   D. intererst

2. I think the _____ packaging of many products is becoming a serious problem.
   A. unecessary
   B. unneccesarry
   C. unnecessary
   D. unnecessarry

Spelling Master 8

attorney	foliage	heir	muscle	society
February	friend	icicles	rhythm	women

▶ Use your own paper to complete the following spelling exercises.

Exercise A: Collecting New Words   Copy the spelling words into your spelling notebook.

Exercise B: Identifying Patterns   Unscramble the letters below to write each spelling word correctly.

1. thrymh
2. fegloia
3. nerfid

4. clumse
5. rihe

Exercise C: Spelling Possessives   For each of the following sentences, write the correct possessive form of the word in parentheses.

1. My favorite element of this song is the (rhythm) strong beat.

2. My (friend) sister belongs to a (women) vocal group.

3. The (heir) inheritance is only enough to cover his (attorney) fees for handling the will.

4. (February) coldness began to fade as the (icicles) drops formed a puddle on the step.

5. It is (society) responsibility to protect the people.

Exercise D: Analyzing Word Origins and Etymologies   Write the spelling word that matches each etymology below.

1. From the Latin word *socius,* meaning "companion"

2. From the Latin word *folium,* meaning "a leaf"

3. From the Latin word *musculus,* meaning "little mouse"

4. From the Old English prefix *īs–,* meaning "ice," and the Old English word *gicel,* meaning "piece of ice"

5. From the Old English prefix *wif–,* meaning "female" and the Old English word *mann,* meaning "human being"

Exercise E: Proofreading   For each group of words below, if one of the words is misspelled, write the letter for that word. If all the words are spelled correctly, write **D** for *No mistake.*

1. A. attorney
   B. Febuary
   C. foliage
   D. No mistake

2. A. friend
   B. society
   C. icycles
   D. No mistake

Spelling Master 9

description	experiment	mathematics	permanent	uncomfortable
exactly	independent	performance	repetition	unusually

▶ Use your own paper to complete the following spelling exercises.

Exercise A: Collecting New Words Copy the spelling words into your spelling notebook.

Exercise B: Recognizing Word Shapes Write the spelling word that matches each shape below.

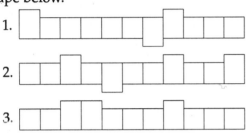

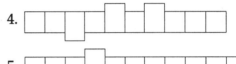

Exercise C: Dividing Words into Syllables Divide the following words into syllables by using slashes to mark the breaks.

1. exactly 2. experiment 3. performance 4. permanent 5. unusually

Exercise D: Spelling Words with Affixes Copy and complete the following chart. Fill in the spelling words that have the affixes listed, and then write in the base word that combines with those affixes to form each spelling word. Finally, determine how the spelling of each base word changed when the affix was added to it.

	Prefix	Spelling Word	Base Word	Suffix
1.	in–			–ent
2.	un–			–able
3.	un–			–ly

Exercise E: Proofreading For each sentence below, if one of the underlined words is misspelled, write the letter for that word. If all the words are spelled correctly, write **D** for *No mistake.*

1. The teaching style of our new <u>mathmatics</u> teacher <u>exactly</u> matched Amelia's

   A   B

   <u>description</u>. <u>No mistake</u>

   C   D

2. At first, I felt <u>uncomfortable</u> working on the <u>independant</u> science <u>experiment</u>.

   A   B   C

   <u>No mistake</u>

   D

Spelling Master 10

aisles	familiar	hungrily	luxury	technique
ceiling	fierce	imaginary	minute	vague

▶ Use your own paper to complete the following spelling exercises.

Exercise A: Collecting New Words   Copy the spelling words into your spelling notebook.

Exercise B: Identifying Patterns   Unscramble the letters below to write each spelling word correctly.

1. slasie
2. gilince
3. chequiten
4. ecrife
5. iraginmay

Exercise C: Spelling Basic Sight Words   Identify and write the word that matches each phonetic spelling.

1. vāg	2. luk'shə rē	3. min'it	4. huŋ'grə lē

Exercise D: Analyzing Word Origins and Etymologies   Write the spelling word that matches each etymology below.

1. From the Latin word *familiaris,* meaning "of a household"
2. From the Old French word *aile,* meaning "wing, section of a building"
3. From the Latin word *luxus,* meaning "extravagance, excess"
4. From the Latin word *ferus,* meaning "wild, savage"
5. From the Old French word *celer,* meaning "to conceal"

Exercise E: Proofreading   For each group of sentences below, if one of the underlined words is misspelled, write the letter for that sentence. If all the words are spelled correctly, write **D** for *No mistake.*

1. A. The plot of the movie seems <u>familar</u>, as if it had been done before.
   B. The judo instructor's <u>technique</u> demonstrated his skills and experience.
   C. One <u>minute</u> before the bell, the teacher returned our assignment.
   D. No mistake

2. A. "I have a <u>fierce</u> headache," stated Manuel during lunch.
   B. I <u>hungerly</u> devoured my sandwich because I had forgotten to eat breakfast.
   C. In my <u>imaginary</u> world, cars would run on vegetable matter, not gas.
   D. No mistake

Practice Test 1

Part 1: Reading Comprehension

Read the following selection, and then complete items 1–5 based on what you read.

THE BASEBALL

In many ways, it's no different from any other baseball. A five-ounce sphere roughly nine inches in circumference. A small piece of cork layered in rubber, yarn, and horsehide. The only difference lies on the surface, where each member of the 1970 Cincinnati Reds scrawled his name in dark-blue ink across pristine white leather pulled tight by thick, red twine.

The colors were once as crisp and sharp as the flag that flew in center field on the brisk fall day that the ball came into my life. But the years have taken their toll. The cover is now yellow and dingy. The seam is starting to separate. The once-supple pebbled surface is now as dry and fragile as parchment. Many of the names have long since faded beyond recognition, but others remain: Johnny Bench, Lee May, Bernie Carbo, Wayne Simpson. Another thing that hasn't faded is the memory.

September, 1970. The Reds were hosting the Los Angeles Dodgers in the final double-header at Crosley Field. Before the year was out, the cozy old ballpark would be torn down and replaced with an enormous, multi-purpose facility with plastic grass and no personality. There was no artificial turf at Crosley Field, just the smell of freshly mown grass, hot dogs, popcorn, and autumn in the air.

In the lull between games, I found the ball at a souvenir stand overflowing with pennants and caps and posters. I wanted that ball more than anything in my ten years on Earth, but it cost five bucks, more money than I could hope to make in a lifetime. I showed it to my uncle, hinting that perhaps he could buy it for me.

"Well," he said, "I suppose I could buy it, but I'll have to keep it myself just to make sure it gets taken care of proper."

I begged and pleaded. I swore that it would never touch the hardwood of a bat or the leather of a glove. But he made me sweat it out for all of game two and all of the three-hour drive home before giving it to me. I tore off the plastic shrink-wrap, tossed the ball in the air, and . . . dropped it. It bounced off my hands, scuffed itself on the concrete carport, and rolled under the car. It was no longer perfect, but it was mine.

The ball sat on top of my bookshelf until a raspberry soda spill left a pink spot the size of a half dollar on one side. That prompted the purchase of a protective plastic case, in which the ball remained even after it ceased to be a prized possession and became, instead, merely a possession. It spent some time in storage, where it picked up a water stain and an inch-long pale-blue crescent that was somebody's autograph before the ink ran. Over the years, the ball has occasionally found itself on display, but it has for the most part been deteriorating in a box or a drawer. Its condition, however, matters less than its ability to call to mind a time and a place that may be gone forever but is never further away than a memory.

---

1. How did the narrator get the baseball?

    A. Lee May threw it to him.

    B. His uncle bought it for him.

    C. He found it in the grass at Crosley Field.

    D. He bought it with his allowance money.

2. What about the baseball makes it special to the writer?

    A. It is still in perfect condition.

    B. It weighs exactly five ounces.

    C. It reminds him of the 1970 Cincinnati Reds.

    D. It reminds him of a happy time in his past.

3. Which of the following words *best* describes the writer's tone in the selection?

    A. carefree

    B. enthusiastic

    C. nostalgic

    D. sad

4. Why does the writer compare the surface of the baseball to parchment?

    A. to help readers imagine how the baseball looks and feels

    B. to help readers imagine how parchment looks and feels

    C. to describe the surface of a brand-new baseball

    D. to describe his memory of the baseball

5. Which of the following excerpts from the selection does *not* contain language that appeals to the senses?

    A. "There was no artificial turf at Crosley Field, just the smell of freshly mown grass, hot dogs, popcorn, and autumn in the air."

    B. ". . . each member of the 1970 Cincinnati Reds scrawled his name in dark-blue ink across pristine white leather . . ."

    C. "The Reds were hosting the Los Angeles Dodgers in the final double-header at Crosley Field."

    D. "The ball sat on top of my bookshelf until a raspberry soda spill left a pink spot the size of a half dollar on one side."

Part 2: Vocabulary

A. For items 6–10, decide which of the four choices has most nearly the opposite meaning of the word given.

6. prudent

    A. cautious

    B. exact

    C. obvious

    D. careless

7. tranquil

    A. noisy

    B. calm

    C. shy

    D. skillful

8. modest

    A. pleasant

    B. boastful

    C. impossible

    D. doubtful

Practice Test 1 *(Continued)*

9. vague

   A. similar

   B. uncertain

   C. clear

   D. ineffective

10. timid

    A. shy

    B. rare

    C. discreet

    D. bold

B. *For items 11–15, use context clues to help determine which word* best *completes each sentence.*

11. The team was disqualified because it had not _____ to the rules of the contest.

    A. confirmed

    B. recommended

    C. distorted

    D. conformed

12. The volunteers not only deserve the award but also _____ our respect.

    A. merit

    B. exclude

    C. adopt

    D. commit

13. After we discussed the impact and probable _____ of the problem, we offered possible solutions.

    A. tactics

    B. effects

    C. calibers

    D. merits

14. *Courage* is an example of a(n) _____ noun, not a concrete noun.

    A. comparable

    B. aerial

    C. abstract

    D. versatile

15. We looked in the car-repair _____ to find out how to change the oil in our car.

    A. myth

    B. manual

    C. satellite

    D. camouflage

Part 3: Spelling

A. *For items 16–20, if one of the underlined words in a sentence is misspelled, write the letter for that word. If all the words are spelled correctly, write **D** for* No mistake.

16. Booing and hissing, the audiance showed
                                   A
    no sympathy for the villain of the play.
       B   C
    No mistake
       D

17. The members of the committee donated
                          A
    ninty dollars to the club's treasury.
      B   C
    No mistake
       D

18. Our candidate became extremly nervous
          A   B   C
    while waiting for the election results.

    No mistake
       D

19. The winner's <u>acceptance</u> <u>speech</u> was <u>breif</u>.
                      A   **B**   **C**

    <u>No mistake</u>
      D

20. Last summer my brother rode his <u>bicycle</u>
                                   A

    <u>across</u> the <u>country</u>. <u>No mistake</u>
     B   **C**   **D**

B. *For items 21–25, write the letter of the word that is spelled correctly and* best *completes each sentence.*

21. Albert Einstein was a mathematical
    _____.

    A. genious

    B. genus

    C. genuis

    D. genius

22. _____, no one was injured in the accident.

    A. Fortunately

    B. Fortunely

    C. Fourtunately

    D. Fortunitely

23. Evidence against the defendant began to
    _____.

    A. accummulate

    B. accumulate

    C. acummulate

    D. acumulate

24. Miss Ramirez helped me _____ the poem.

    A. intrepert

    B. interpretate

    C. interpret

    D. intepret

25. I sent Mother a _____ of sunflowers.

    A. boquet

    B. bouquet

    C. bowquet

    D. booquay

Practice Test 2

Part 1: Reading Comprehension

Read the following selection, and then complete items 1–5 based on what you read.

DANIEL AND THE DOBERMAN

Daniel felt a hand gently shake his shoulder.

"You better get moving," his mother said. "You're going to be late again!"

Blinking groggily, Daniel sat up in bed, rubbed the sleep from his eyes, and ran his fingers through his short, dark hair. The bed-side clock told him that his mother was right. He had better get going.

He showered and dressed in baggy jeans, a T-shirt, and sneakers, then grabbed his backpack and rushed to the kitchen.

"Hi, Mom," Daniel said as he passed through the kitchen. He picked up his lunch box and grabbed some fruit. "Bye, Mom," he said on his way out the back door.

Daniel walked down the sidewalk of his quiet neighborhood. He stopped and checked his watch. School started in seven minutes. He had no choice. He would have to take the shortcut.

To the neighborhood kids, the shortcut meant just one thing: The Monster.

The Monster was the Stockton's Doberman pinscher, a vicious, snarling beast that, according to one story, had once eaten a third-grader. Having encountered the beast, Daniel didn't doubt the story. He himself might have been a doggie treat if not for the rope that tethered the dog to a large oak tree.

Daniel stood at the corner for a moment, trying to think of another option. He shook his head. "I can't be late again," he thought.

So he headed across the street, and hopped a fence into the Martinson's back yard. Mr. Martinson, a retired mail carrier, looked up from his gardening.

"Mornin' Daniel," he said. "Late again?"

"Yes, sir," Daniel said.

"You get moving then." Daniel did just that.

He hopped another fence and trotted down a utility access area between two fenced-in back yards. As he approached the Stockton's back yard, he slowed down and briefly considered going back.

"I can't be late," he thought.

He took a running start and hopped the fence into the Stockton's back yard. As Daniel cleared the fence, The Monster looked up from where it lay among the coiled-up rope near the oak tree. Daniel thought he could detect the slightest hint of a smile on The Monster's muzzle, as though it were pleased by the thought of this unexpected snack.

Daniel swallowed hard and took a step backward. "Animals can sense fear," he said to himself, "so just be brave."

The Monster stood up and licked its lips.

"I'm not afraid of you," Daniel said.

Daniel started to move his right foot forward. Suddenly, The Monster was charging, kicking up loose rocks and dirt behind him. Daniel tore off at top speed for the fence about fifty feet away. The Monster was gaining, but Daniel wasn't too worried. Any minute now, the leash would snap taut and the dog would be jerked to a stop.

Daniel hopped up on the fence and turned back so he could watch The Monster reach the end of its leash. At first, Daniel was confused. The Monster seemed much closer than usual this time. Then he saw the rope, still coiled up neatly at the base of the oak tree.

By then, it was too late.

"No!" Daniel screamed and covered his face. The Monster leaped at him and knocked him to the ground. "No!" Daniel curled into a ball and waited for the Monster to sink its teeth into his flesh.

What he felt, instead, was the dog's wet, sloppy tongue. The dog licked his face again.

"Hey!" Daniel said, laughing. "Cut it out!"

Practice Test 2 (Continued)

1. At the beginning of the story, Daniel is

   A. fighting

   B. playing a video game

   C. sleeping

   D. looking for The Monster

2. Which of the following statements is *not* supported by the details of the story?

   A. Daniel is occasionally late for school.

   B. The Monster once ate one of Daniel's friends.

   C. Daniel has taken the shortcut before.

   D. The Monster appears to be a vicious creature.

3. Why does Daniel take the shortcut?

   A. to speak to Mr. Martinson

   B. to play with The Monster

   C. to return a video game

   D. to avoid being late for school

4. In an effort to prevent The Monster from attacking him, Daniel

   A. gives The Monster a doggie treat

   B. crawls quietly through Mr. Stockton's back yard

   C. acts as if he were not afraid of The Monster

   D. tosses The Monster a chewed-up tennis ball

5. Based on the outcome of the story, readers may conclude that Daniel

   A. will no longer fear The Monster

   B. will always take the shortcut

   C. will continue to believe that The Monster once ate a third-grader

   D. will never be late for school again

Part 2: Vocabulary

A. *For items 6–10, decide which of the four choices has most nearly the* same *meaning as the italicized word in each phrase.*

6. a *hostile* environment

   A. natural

   B. positive

   C. pleasant

   D. unfriendly

7. an *abrupt* change

   A. peaceful

   B. sudden

   C. incredible

   D. essential

8. an *illustrious* career

   A. distinguished

   B. uncertain

   C. financial

   D. industrious

9. a *vital* ingredient

   A. missing

   B. unknown

   C. necessary

   D. tiny

10. *diverse* opinions

    A. specific

    B. different

    C. important

    D. favorable

B. *For items 11–16, use context clues to help determine which word* best *completes each sentence.*

11. The train is traveling at a _____ of 90 miles per hour.
    A. magnitude
    B. velocity
    C. precaution
    D. flaw

12. The writer sent copies of her _____ to several publishers.
    A. blemish
    B. capacity
    C. manuscript
    D. overture

13. Once the arena has reached its _____, we cannot admit anyone else.
    A. phase
    B. kernel
    C. endurance
    D. capacity

14. The Richter scale is used to measure the _____ of an earthquake.
    A. magnitude
    B. undergrowth
    C. habitat
    D. prestige

15. The invention of the word processor seems to have made the typewriter _____.
    A. stationary
    B. obsolete
    C. indispensable
    D. notorious

Part 3: Spelling
A. *For items 16–20, if one of the underlined words in a sentence is misspelled, write the letter for that sentence. If all the words are spelled correctly, write **D** for No mistake.*

16. A. One of the president's duties is to execute the laws.
    B. The icicles are melting.
    C. Who is the hair to the British throne?
    D. No mistake

17. A. The scientists conducted the experiment.
    B. Is a strait line the shortest distance between two points?
    C. Jorge is my best friend.
    D. No mistake

18. A. Grades are a part of a student's permanent record.
    B. You should receive the package on Friday.
    C. The students showed much intrest in the project.
    D. No mistake

Practice Test 2 (Continued)

19. A. The class discussed the rhyme and <u>rhythm</u> of the poem.

    B. <u>Who's</u> bicycle is this?

    C. I am not <u>familiar</u> with these words.

    D. No mistake

20. A. He did <u>exactly</u> what he was supposed to do.

    B. The figure skater's <u>performance</u> was flawless.

    C. A huge piñata hung from the center of the <u>ceiling</u>.

    D. No mistake

B. *For items 21–25, write the letter of the word that is spelled correctly and best completes each sentence.*

21. Each _____ addressed the jury.

    A. attornie

    B. attourney

    C. attorney

    D. atturney

22. William has _____ to another school.

    A. transferred

    B. transfered

    C. transfferred

    D. transeferred

23. There is only one _____ left in the game.

    A. minit

    B. minnit

    C. minutte

    D. minute

24. Are you going to the movie _____?

    A. twonight

    B. too-night

    C. tonight

    D. tonite

25. My little brother has an _____ friend.

    A. immaginary

    B. imaginery

    C. immaginarry

    D. imaginary

Teaching Notes

READING MASTER 1

In this master, students will demonstrate basic comprehension of the excerpt from "Questions and Answers," identify supporting details, identify problem-solution relationships, identify the author's viewpoint, and evaluate source credibility and reliability.

1. Extend item 1 by discussing with students some reasons that an experienced person would want to help a person who was interested in or just starting out in a particular field.
2. Discuss with students the difference between books and periodicals. You might want to bring to class examples of books and periodicals that contain poems.
3. After students have completed item 3, you may want to have them list examples of clichés that they should try to avoid in their writing.
4. To assist students with item 4, suggest that they look for evidence in the selection to support each of the answer choices.
5. Remind students that there are many good readers of literary texts and that a person would not have to be an expert to enjoy poetry. Randall's experience as an editor and publisher, however, would make him an expert, professional reader of poetry.

READING MASTER 2

In this master, students will demonstrate basic comprehension of the excerpt from *Black Elk Speaks*, scan the selection for specific information, identify sequence of events, identify the author's tone, and make inferences.

1. In responding to item 1, students might describe a specific incident within the selection, or they might give a general overview of Black Elk's experience in the Wild West Show.
2. Remind students that scanning is a helpful strategy for finding specific information without reading or re-reading an entire text. Ask students what word or words they might scan for to find the answer to this item.
3. This excerpt is organized in chronological, or time, order. Before students begin item 3, ask them to identify signals of chronological order in the selection, such as *first, then,* and *after that.*
4. Have students point out evidence of Black Elk's attitude toward Queen Victoria, such as that given in the third and final paragraphs.
5. Explain that when Black Elk says "it would have been better," he alludes to his people's recent history, in which families were disrupted and removed from their ancestral homes.

READING MASTER 3

In this master, students will preview "The Spaceport Mermaids," demonstrate basic comprehension, identify

cause-and-effect relationships, make inferences, and identify the main idea.

1. Complete item 1 with the whole class. Ask students to share what they know about the Kennedy Space Center, mermaids, and manatees. How might the three be connected?
2. In order to focus their reading, have students preview item 2 before they read the selection.
3. To assist students with item 3, explain that *cause* makes something happen, and *effect* is what happens. Writers often use specific words to signal cause-and-effect relationships, such as *because, as a result,* and *therefore.* Point out that the cause-and-effect relationship in this selection is spread over several paragraphs.
4. Explain that writers often make a point without stating it directly and that readers have to use the information presented to make an inference about what the writer is trying to say. If students have trouble with this item, guide them with questions such as "Why does NASA use special boats in waters inhabited by manatees? How might a propeller be dangerous to manatees? Why might a water jet be less dangerous to manatees?"
5. Explain that the main idea is the most important thing a writer claims or argues in a selection. In a multiple-choice item such as this one, one way to determine the main idea is to compare the amount of support for each of the four answer choices. The answer choice that has the most support in the selection is likely to be the main idea of the selection.

READING MASTER 4

In this master, students will demonstrate basic comprehension of "The Jacket," identify sequence of events, identify figurative language, make inferences, and identify the main idea.

1. In order to focus their reading, have students preview item 1 before they read the selection.
2. This autobiographical incident is organized in chronological order. To assist students with this item, have them scan the selection for signals of chronological order, such as "the next day" and "that winter."
3. To answer item 3, students may need some explanation of personification. Explain that personification is a kind of metaphor in which a nonhuman thing, like a jacket, is talked about as if it were a human. The selection contains other examples of personification you can point out to students or have them identify.
4. To answer item 4, students must recognize the use of figurative language and make an inference based on what they have read. If students have

Teaching Notes (Continued)

trouble with this item, guide them with questions such as "Why does the boy say the jacket is like an ugly brother? How do you think that makes him feel? What does the boy mean by 'that day and ever since'?"
5. Remind students that the main idea is the most important thing a writer claims or argues for or against in a selection. In this story, the main idea is stated in the opening paragraph and again in the last paragraph.

READING MASTER 5

In this master, students will demonstrate basic comprehension of the excerpt from *Nisei Daughter*, identify sensory language, interpret figurative language, identify the author's purpose, and identify the author's tone.

1. To extend this item, facilitate a class discussion of favorite foods. Are students' favorite foods special because the foods come from a certain culture, because someone special makes them, or simply because they taste good?
2. Explain that sensory language can help writers paint in a reader's mind a vivid picture of an object or event.
3. Explain that using figurative language is another way that writers express themselves vividly. In this selection, the writer uses several similes, or comparisons of unlike things using *like* or *as*, to create strong visual images of the foods she is describing. To extend this item, have students make up some similes on their own.
4. Students should recognize that this is an example of descriptive writing in which the author is expressing personal feelings or thoughts. To review the purposes, or aims, of writing, see page 7 in the Pupil's Edition.
5. Remind students that the tone of a selection reflects the author's attitude toward the subject. After students have completed this item, have them cite specific evidence from the selection that led to their answers.

READING MASTER 6

In this master, students will make predictions about "Coyote Places the Stars," demonstrate basic comprehension, scan for specific information, identify sequence of events, and draw conclusions.

1. Have students complete item 1 as a class. Make a class list of predictions. After students have read the selection, go back over the list to see which predictions were most accurate.
2. To extend item 2, bring to class pictures of the Big Dipper and discuss how this constellation is related to the story.

3. Before students begin item 3, have them think briefly about what word or words they will scan for to determine the answer to this question. In order to choose the correct response, students will have to recognize that one coyote, five wolves, and one dog climb the arrow ladder.
4. This folk tale is organized in chronological order. To assist students with this item, have them scan the selection for signals of chronological order, such as "next evening" and "for many days."
5. Extend item 5 by asking students to discuss what Coyote's words and actions suggest about his character.

READING MASTER 7

In this master, students will activate prior knowledge of the subject matter of "How to Eat Like a Child," demonstrate basic comprehension, scan for specific information, outline, and make inferences.

1. Have pairs of students complete item 1 together, and then have each pair share their instructions with the class.
2. In order to focus their reading, have students preview item 2 before they read the selection.
3. Before students begin item 3, have them think briefly about what word or words they will scan for to determine the answer to this question.
4. Explain that an outline is the organizing of a selection into topics, subtopics, and supporting information. To complete this outline, students must determine which of the choices is supporting information for the subtopic, "Eating an Ice-Cream Cone."
5. After students have completed item 5, extend the item by asking students to point out some of the details they think are the most humorous.

READING MASTER 8

In this master, students will preview the advertisement, demonstrate basic comprehension, identify the author's purpose, draw conclusions, and identify persuasive techniques.

1. Extend this item by discussing with students their first impressions of the advertisement. Do they find it interesting? Do they want to read the smaller print to see what the ad is about?
2. To extend item 2, have students describe other print, radio, or television ads that promote similar products.
3. After students have completed item 3 and have recognized that the advertisement is an example of persuasive writing, discuss the fact that readers must be aware of the writer's purpose in order to evaluate the objectivity of any piece of writing.

Teaching Notes (Continued)

4. After students have completed this item, discuss how the success of this advertisement depends on the reader's being able to draw the conclusion that milk is a good source of potassium. Extend the item by having students tell what in the advertisement led them to this conclusion.
5. To review some of the persuasive techniques commonly used in advertising, see pages 268–269 in the Pupil's Edition.

READING MASTER 9

In this master, students will demonstrate basic comprehension of the review of Lois Lowry's *Number the Stars*, identify the main idea, draw conclusions, identify the author's tone, and distinguish fact from opinion.

1. Have the class work together to complete item 1. Draw the T-chart on the chalkboard, and fill it in with the information students provide.
2. In order to focus their reading, have students preview item 2 before they read.
3. To assist students with item 3, explain that all of the answer choices are factually correct but that only one represents a conclusion that can be drawn from the information given.
4. Remind students that the tone of a selection reflects the author's attitude toward the subject. After students have completed this item, have them cite specific evidence from the selection that led to their answers.
5. When students read a critical review, they must be able to distinguish the reviewer's personal opinions from actual facts about the work being reviewed. To extend item 5, go through the brief review sentence by sentence with the class and have students determine whether each sentence is a statement of fact or opinion.

READING MASTER 10

In this master, students will demonstrate basic comprehension of the excerpt from *Meet-a-Cheetah*, identify comparison and contrast relationships, distinguish fact from opinion, identify supporting details, and summarize the selection's main argument.

1. In order to focus their reading, have students preview item 1 before they read the selection.
2. Explain that comparison shows how things are alike and that contrast shows how things are different. Before students begin item 2, have them identify signals of comparison and contrast in the selection, such as *like* (comparison) and *rather* (contrast).
3. Remind students that a statement of fact contains information that can be proved to be true. It contains objective information about things that happened in the past or are happening in the

present. A statement of opinion, on the other hand, expresses a personal belief or attitude. Students must distinguish between fact and opinion to make judgments about what they read.
4. Remind students that supporting details explain, prove, or expand on the main idea of a selection. Supporting details may include facts, reasons, examples, sensory details, and quotations.
5. Explain that summarizing means restating the main ideas expressed in a piece of writing. In a multiple-choice item, students can determine which answer choice best summarizes a selection by determining which one addresses all of the most important points in the selection.

VOCABULARY MASTER 1

In this master, students will copy ten new vocabulary words and their definitions, analyze word parts, use context clues to complete a paragraph, use vocabulary words in a report, and select synonyms for vocabulary words.

adopt	ə däpt′	recommend	rek′ə mend′
anguish	aŋ′gwish	subtle	sut″l
exclude	eks klo͞od′	supervise	so͞o′pər vīz′
infrequent	in frē′kwənt	tactics	tak′tiks
prudent	pro͞od′ ′nt	turmoil	tʉr′moil′

Exercise A Have students write each word in the context of a sentence to aid in comprehension and retention.

Exercise B Before assigning this exercise, review with students the different types of word parts: roots, prefixes, and suffixes. Roots contain the core meaning of the word. Prefixes and suffixes are word parts that affect the meaning and can change the part of speech of the root to which they are attached. In *replay*, *–play–* is a root and *re–* is a prefix.

Before beginning Exercise B, go over the analysis of the word *recommend*. After students have identified the prefix *re–* and the root *–commend–*, have them give examples of other words with the same prefix. From their examples, have students develop a definition of the prefix *re–*, as well as of the root *–commend–*. Either model for students or have them explain in their own words how the parts (prefix and root) combine to form the new word, and what change in meaning occurred. To review common prefixes and suffixes, see pages 861–862 in the Pupil's Edition.

Exercise C Explain to students that although other vocabulary words could complete each sentence grammatically, only one word makes sense given the context of the sentence. Students should examine the idea expressed in each sentence and then choose the word that both completes and supports the context. To review different types of context clues, see page 863 in the Pupil's Edition.

Teaching Notes (Continued)

Exercise D Stress to students the importance of experimenting with new vocabulary words in a variety of contexts, especially in their everyday interactions. Explain that a good way to remember new words is to use them frequently, and that the ability to find the appropriate and accurate words to express oneself in various "real-life" situations demonstrates a person's communication skills and literacy.

Exercise E These items are designed to give students practice selecting synonyms, a skill frequently required on standardized tests.

VOCABULARY MASTER 2

In this master, students will copy ten new vocabulary words and their definitions, connect the origins of words with their modern meanings, respond to questions involving vocabulary words, determine whether vocabulary words are used correctly, and select synonyms for vocabulary words.

aerial	er′ē əl	**offend**	ə fend′
destiny	des′tə nē	**repel**	ri pel′
edible	ed′ə bəl	**timid**	tim′id
eloquent	el′ə kwənt	**tutor**	tōōt′ər
motive	mōt′iv	**versatile**	vur′sə təl

Exercise A Have students write each word in the context of a sentence to aid in comprehension and retention.

Exercise B Etymology is the study of the origins and development of words. Tell students that in addition to being interesting, knowing the origin of a word can often help them better understand the word's meaning by giving it a historical or geographic context. Also, knowing how a word's meaning has changed over time can help the student understand the word's usage in a variety of contexts.

Demonstrate how to complete this exercise by giving the following etymology: "From the Greek prefix *archi–*, meaning 'chief' and the Greek *tekton*, meaning 'carpenter.'" Students will probably be able to identify the contemporary word *architect* based on the etymology. Then demonstrate how to reason out how the word's origin might have led to its modern definition. For example, while *architect* used to mean the chief carpenter of a building, the meaning has expanded to signify someone whose profession is designing and supervising the construction of buildings.

Exercise C You might introduce or extend this exercise by calling on students to respond orally to similar questions using some of the other vocabulary words.

Exercise D Tell students that *denotation* is another name for the objective dictionary definition of a word. Students should compare the way the vocabulary word is used in each sentence with the word's definition at the top of the master.

Exercise E These items are designed to give students practice selecting synonyms, a skill frequently required on standardized tests.

VOCABULARY MASTER 3

In this master, students will copy ten new vocabulary words and their definitions, analyze words with Greek and Latin roots, determine alternate meanings of words, relate dictionary definitions to given contexts, and select antonyms of vocabulary words.

abstract	ab strakt′	**gratify**	grat′i fī′
caliber	kal′ə bər	**impact**	im′pakt′
conform	kən fôrm′	**incredible**	in kred′ə bəl
elaborate	ē lab′ə rit	**manual**	man′yōō əl
grammatical	grə mat′i kəl	**modest**	mäd′ist

Exercise A Have students write each word in the context of a sentence to aid in comprehension and retention.

Exercise B Since a majority of English words come either directly or indirectly from Greek and Latin, a familiarity with Greek and Latin roots and their meanings can help students decipher the meanings of hundreds of unfamiliar words. Illustrate this point by naming a common root such as *–log–* ("speech, word") and naming or asking students to name words using that root (*dialogue, monologue*). To review information about roots, see page 861 in the Pupil's Edition.

Exercise C Advise students to carefully examine the context of the sentences to determine the alternate meanings of the vocabulary words. In some cases, there may be a logical connection between the new definition and the one given in the vocabulary list; ask students to look for and explain these connections. Suggest that students use a dictionary to check their definitions.

Exercise D If students are having difficulty identifying which dictionary definition corresponds to a sentence, suggest that they substitute the different definitions for the vocabulary word to determine which definition best maintains the sentence's original meaning.

Exercise E These items are designed to give students practice selecting antonyms, a skill frequently required on standardized tests. Remind students that they should look for the word that has the *opposite* meaning of the vocabulary word.

VOCABULARY MASTER 4

In this master, students will copy ten new vocabulary words and their definitions, research the origins of vocabulary words, use context clues to complete a paragraph, show relationships among word families, and select synonyms of vocabulary words.

Teaching Notes *(Continued)*

aggravate	ag′rə vāt′	**excess**	ek ses′
commit	kə mit′	**ignorance**	ig′nə rəns
comparable	käm′pə rə bəl	**irritable**	ir′i tə bəl
confirm	kən fʉrm′	**recognition**	rek′əg nish′ən
distort	di stôrt′	**veto**	vē′tō

Exercise A   Have students write each word in the context of a sentence to aid in comprehension and retention.

Exercise B   Extend this activity by having students research the origins of other vocabulary words from this master.

Exercise C   Remind students that this exercise will sometimes require them to change the form of a vocabulary word to match the structure of the sentence. They might have to make a singular noun or verb plural, or add –ed or –ing to a verb to put it in the appropriate tense. Students should be prepared to identify the context clues that help them determine which word best completes each sentence. To review different types of context clues, see page 863 in the Pupil's Edition.

Exercise D   Understanding the relationships between words that share the same root will help students to learn several new words for every word that appears on a vocabulary list. Allow students who are having difficulty to work with a partner or to consult a dictionary in completing this exercise.

Exercise E   These items are designed to give students practice selecting synonyms, a skill frequently required on standardized tests.

VOCABULARY MASTER 5

In this master, students will copy ten new vocabulary words and their definitions, research the origins of words from other languages, describe connotations of vocabulary words, use vocabulary words to write a letter, and select synonyms of vocabulary words.

camouflage	kam′ə fläzh′	**notable**	nōt′ə bəl
effect	e fekt′	**ridicule**	rid′i kyōol′
loiter	loit′ər	**satellite**	sat′'l īt′
merit	mer′it	**tranquil**	tran′kwil
myth	mith	**vague**	vāg

Exercise A   Have students write each word in the context of a sentence to aid in comprehension and retention.

Exercise B   Show students where to find a word's etymology in the dictionary and how to read the abbreviations and symbols used in an etymology. Students can look up unfamiliar abbreviations in the dictionary's abbreviation key, often found inside the front or back cover. To review a sample dictionary entry including etymology information, see page 857 in the Pupil's Edition.

Exercise C   Explain the differences between denotation and connotation. A word's *denotation* is its objective dictionary definition. Its *connotation* is made up of the ideas, notions, associations, and overtones suggested by the word. For example, the main character in a story may be described as *proud* or as *arrogant*. The words have similar denotative meanings, but they suggest different ideas. *Proud* can suggest self-respect and a sense of accomplishment. *Arrogant*, on the other hand, has negative connotations of snobbishness, or a superior attitude. In this exercise, students are asked to describe their connotations of the vocabulary words, based on context. Students' associations and positive or negative ideas about the words will depend on their perceptions and personal experiences.

Exercise D   This activity requires students to build upon their understanding of some of the vocabulary words by using them in the realistic context of writing a letter of recommendation for a friend.

Exercise E   These items are designed to give students practice selecting synonyms, a skill frequently required on standardized tests.

VOCABULARY MASTER 6

In this master, students will copy ten new vocabulary words and their definitions, analyze the origins of words with Greek and Latin roots, use context clues to choose among homonyms, respond to questions involving vocabulary words, and select antonyms of vocabulary words.

dual	dōō′əl	**manuscript**	man′yōo skript′
geological	jē′ə läj′ik əl	**phase**	fāz
hostile	häs′təl	**propel**	prō pel′
intermediate	in′tər mē′dē it	**stationary**	stā′shə ner′ē
kernel	kʉr′nəl	**submerged**	sub mʉrj″d

Exercise A   Have students write each word in the context of a sentence to aid in comprehension and retention.

Exercise B   To review information about roots, see page 861 in the Pupil's Edition.

Exercise C   Tell students that a homonym is a word that has the same pronunciation as another word, but with a different meaning and usually a different spelling. To expand on this activity, have students write definitions for the four words in the exercise that are homonyms of vocabulary words.

Exercise D   Introduce or extend this exercise by calling on students to respond orally to similar questions using some of the other vocabulary words.

Exercise E   These items are designed to give students practice selecting antonyms, a skill frequently required in standardized tests. Remind students that they should look for the word that has the *opposite* meaning of the vocabulary word.

Teaching Notes *(Continued)*

VOCABULARY MASTER 7

In this master, students will copy ten new vocabulary words and their definitions, research technical and specialized meanings of words, use vocabulary words in a letter to the editor, relate dictionary definitions to given contexts, and select synonyms of vocabulary words.

banish	ban′ish	obsolete	äb′sə lēt′
flaw	flô	overture	o′vər chər
habitat	hab′i tat′	radiate	rā′dē āt′
immune	im myōōn′	refrain	ri frān′
magnitude	mag′nə tōōd′	speculate	spek′yōō lāt′

Exercise A Have students write each word in the context of a sentence to aid in comprehension and retention.

Exercise B To expand on this exercise, ask students to name other words they are familiar with from the fields of music and astronomy, or other words that have both general and specialized meanings.

Exercise C This activity requires students to build upon their understanding of some of the vocabulary words by using them to write a letter to the editor discussing their opinions on hunting for food.

Exercise D Remind students that a word's denotation is its objective dictionary definition. Students should compare the way the vocabulary word is used in each sentence with the definition at the top of the page.

Exercise E These items are designed to give students practice selecting synonyms, a skill frequently required on standardized tests.

VOCABULARY MASTER 8

In this master, students will copy ten new vocabulary words and their definitions, analyze word parts, discuss connotations of vocabulary words, use context clues to complete a paragraph, and select synonyms for vocabulary words.

abrupt	ə brupt′	indispensable	
capacity	kə pas′i tē		in′ di spen′sə bəl
endurance	en door′ əns	maternal	mə tur′nəl
hysterical	hi ster′i kəl	pivot	piv′ət
illustrious	i lus′trē əs	prestige	pres tēzh′
		revise	ri vīz′

Exercise A Have students write each word in the context of a sentence to aid in comprehension and retention.

Exercise B Go over the analysis of the word *endurance* with your students before they do the remaining words in the exercise. Extend the exercise by having students brainstorm other words with the same roots or affixes. To review common prefixes and suffixes, see pages 861–862 in the Pupil's Edition.

Exercise C Remind students that a word's denotation is its objective dictionary definition, while a word's connotation includes other ideas, notions, associations, and overtones suggested by the word.

Exercise D Tell students that they should be prepared to identify the context clues that help them determine which word best completes each sentence. To review different types of context clues, see page 863 in the Pupil's Edition.

Exercise E Theses items are designed to give students practice selecting synonyms, a skill frequently required on standardized tests.

VOCABULARY MASTER 9

In this master, students will copy ten new vocabulary words and their definitions, research the origins of vocabulary words, show relationships among word families, respond to questions involving vocabulary words, and select antonyms of vocabulary words.

audible	ô′də bəl	fascinate	fas′ə nāt′
avert	ə vurt′	inferior	in fir′ē ər
blemish	blem′ish	invade	in vād′
diverse	də vurs′	patron	pā′trən
expand	ek spand′	vital	vīt′′l

Exercise A Have students write each word in the context of a sentence to aid in comprehension and retention.

Exercise B Extend this activity by having students research the origins of other vocabulary words from this master.

Exercise C Have students check their answers in a dictionary after completing this exercise.

Exercise D Introduce or extend this exercise by calling on students to respond orally to similar questions using some of the other vocabulary words.

Exercise E These items are designed to give students practice selecting antonyms, a skill frequently required on standardized tests. Remind students that they should look for the word that has the *opposite* meaning of the vocabulary word.

VOCABULARY MASTER 10

In this master, students will copy ten new vocabulary words and their definitions, analyze words with Greek and Latin roots, analyze compound words, use vocabulary words to plan a story, and select synonyms of vocabulary words.

Teaching Notes (Continued)

contemplate	kän'təm plāt'	pursue	pər sōō'
intolerable	in täl'ər ə bəl	self-conscious	self kän'shəs
legible	lej'ə bəl	undergrowth	un'dər grōth'
notorious	nō tôr'ē əs	velocity	və läs'ə tē
precaution	prē kô'shən	zoology	zō äl'ə jē

Exercise A Have students write each word in the context of a sentence to aid in comprehension and retention.

Exercise B To review information about roots, see page 861 in the Pupil's Edition.

Exercise C Tell students that a compound word is a single word that is made up of two individual words. Compounds can be closed, as in *undergrowth*; hyphenated, as in *self-conscious*; or open, as in *high school*.

Exercise D This activity requires students to build upon their understanding of some of the vocabulary words by using them in the realistic context of planning the details of a mystery story.

Exercise E These items are designed to give students practice selecting synonyms, a skill frequently required on standardized tests.

SPELLING MASTER 1

In this master, students will write ten new spelling words correctly, identify words with the /e/ sound, divide words into syllables, analyze the spelling of words with suffixes, and identify spelling errors in sentences.

Exercise A You may want to administer a pretest before handing out Spelling Master 1. Have students divide a piece of paper into two columns and number the left-hand column from 1 to 10. Dictate the spelling words to students, providing context by using each word in a sentence. Have students write each word in the left column of the page as it is dictated. Then, using the word list from Spelling Master 1, have students check their own work and write each word correctly in the right-hand column.

Exercise B Ask students to identify how many different ways the /e/ sound is spelled in their spelling words. Make a list of the different spellings on the chalkboard. To extend this exercise, have students brainstorm other words that contain the /e/ sound.

Exercise C Remind students that a dictionary is a good resource that shows how words should be divided into syllables. For additional practice dividing words into syllables, see page 765 in the Pupil's Edition.

Exercise D Explain to students that an affix—a suffix or a prefix—is a small word part that has meaning and can change the definition and the original spelling of a base word. Model Exercise D for students, using the word *acknowledgment*. Show students that *acknowledgment* is made up of the word *acknowledge* and the suffix

–ment. Then model for students or have them explain in their own words how the parts combine to form the new word and what, if any, changes in spelling occur. To review basic rules for spelling words with affixes, see pages 769–771 in the Pupil's Edition.

Exercise E These items help students learn to recognize spelling errors in context.

SPELLING MASTER 2

In this master, students will write ten new spelling words correctly, spell basic sight words based on their phonetic spellings, change singular nouns into their plural forms, analyze word origins and etymologies, and identify spelling errors in sentences.

Exercise A You may want to administer a pretest before handing out Spelling Master 2. See Teaching Notes for Spelling Master 1 for instructions.

Exercise B If students are not familiar with the phonetic alphabet, review with them the pronunciation key and phonetic symbols in a dictionary or on page 935 in the Pupil's Edition. Model how to sound out a word's pronunciation. Before beginning this activity, have students look up one or two of their spelling words to see how they are represented phonetically. For a sample dictionary entry including pronunciation information, see page 857 in the Pupil's Edition.

Exercise C Students may benefit from dividing these words into groups according to how their plurals are formed. Draw a chart with three columns on the chalkboard and label the columns *–s*, *–es*, and *–ies*, respectively. Have volunteers tell you in which column each spelling word belongs. Then have students generate some rules for spelling plurals based on these groupings. To review the rules for spelling the plurals of nouns, see pages 773–776 in the Pupil's Edition.

Exercise D Explain that etymology is the study of the origin and development of words. By becoming familiar with a word's etymology, students can recognize similar words with the same root. Use the word *knowledge* to show students how to analyze the etymology of a word. Prior to beginning this exercise, you may also want to show students how to identify the etymological information in a dictionary entry. For a sample dictionary entry including etymological information, see page 857 in the Pupil's Edition.

Exercise E These items help students learn to recognize spelling errors in context.

SPELLING MASTER 3

In this master, students will write ten new spelling words correctly, identify words containing the /ə/ sound, spell contractions, analyze the spelling of words with suffixes, and choose the correct spellings of words in context.

Teaching Notes (Continued)

Exercise A You may want to administer a pretest before handing out Spelling Master 3. See Teaching Notes for Spelling Master 1 for instructions.

Exercise B Ask students to identify how many different ways the /ə/ sound is spelled in their spelling words. To extend this exercise, have students brainstorm other words with the /ə/ sound.

Exercise C To review basic rules for forming contractions, see pages 749–750 in the Pupil's Edition.

Exercise D Model this exercise with other words that allow suffixes to be added to them, such as *circulate* → *circulation*. To review basic rules for spelling words with affixes, see pages 769–771 in the Pupil's Edition.

Exercise E These items help students learn to choose the correct spelling of a word in context.

SPELLING MASTER 4

In this master, students will write ten new spelling words correctly, identify consonant combinations within words, spell basic sight words based on their phonetic spellings, identify words based on their shapes, and identify spelling errors in sentences.

Exercise A You may want to administer a pretest before handing out Spelling Master 4. See Teaching Notes for Spelling Master 1 for instructions.

Exercise B Explain that sometimes each letter in a consonant combination is pronounced individually, as in *responsibility;* sometimes the combination is pronounced as a new sound for which no single letter exists, as in *machine;* and sometimes one or more of the letters in the combination is silent, as in *campaign.*

Exercise C Before beginning this activity, you may want to have students look up one or two of their spelling words in the dictionary to see how they are represented phonetically. For a key to the pronunciation symbols used in this exercise, see page 935 in the Pupil's Edition.

Exercise D Recognizing word shapes is a basic visual exercise that focuses on the shapes of letters that make up a word. To model this exercise, choose a spelling word from this master, such as *privilege,* and have students outline the shape of each letter with a box.

Exercise E These items help students learn to recognize spelling errors in context.

SPELLING MASTER 5

In this master, students will write ten new spelling words correctly, unscramble letters to write spelling words, divide words into syllables, analyze word origins and etymologies, and identify misspelled words.

Exercise A You may want to administer a pretest before handing out Spelling Master 5. See Teaching Notes for Spelling Master 1 for instructions.

Exercise B Unscrambling letters to write spelling words is a fun way for students to practice recognizing common letter patterns. If students enjoy practicing spelling with puzzles and games, encourage them to make up their own. For example, students can construct word search puzzles that incorporate spelling words spelled both correctly and incorrectly. Classmates then attempt to identify the words, circling the words that are spelled correctly and crossing out those spelled incorrectly.

Exercise C Remind students that a dictionary is a good resource that shows how words should be divided into syllables. For additional practice dividing words into syllables, see page 765 in the Pupil's Edition.

Exercise D To extend this exercise, challenge students to come up with and spell words that share any of the word parts featured in this activity. For example, *fortune* also comes from the Latin word *fortuna.*

Exercise E These items help students learn to identify misspelled words in a list.

SPELLING MASTER 6

In this master, students will write ten new spelling words correctly, identify the spelling words that contain the consonant combination *gh,* identify words based on their shapes, choose the correct homonyms to complete sentences, and identify spelling errors in sentences.

Exercise A You may want to administer a pretest before handing out Spelling Master 6. See Teaching Notes for Spelling Master 1 for instructions.

Exercise B Ask students how many different sounds are produced in the spelling words by the consonant combination *gh.* To extend this exercise, you may want to have students brainstorm other words with the consonant combination *gh.*

Exercise C To model this exercise, choose a spelling word from this master and have students outline the shape of each letter with a box. Spelling is a highly visual skill, and students will benefit from activities that require them to recognize and analyze the shapes of words.

Exercise D The spellings of homonyms are often confused. For students who have problems in this area, you may want to recommend that they keep a list of these words and definitions to refer to when they write.

Exercise E These items help students learn to recognize spelling errors in context.

SPELLING MASTER 7

In this master, students will write ten new spelling words correctly, identify spelling words that contain the /ē/ sound, identify missing letters in spelling words, proofread a paragraph for spelling errors, and choose the correct spelling of words in context.

Teaching Notes (Continued)

Exercise A You may want to administer a pretest before handing out Spelling Master 7. See Teaching Notes for Spelling Master 1 for instructions.

Exercise B Ask students to identify how many different ways the /ē/ sound is spelled in their spelling words. You may want to make a list of the different spellings on the chalkboard. To extend this exercise, have students brainstorm other words that contain the /ē/ sound.

Exercise C Spelling is a highly visual skill, and students will benefit from activities that require them to recognize the patterns of vowels and consonants in words.

Exercise D This exercise helps students practice their proofreading skills by recognizing spelling errors in context.

Exercise E These items help students learn to choose the correct spelling of a word in context.

SPELLING MASTER 8

In this master, students will write ten new spelling words correctly, unscramble letters to write spelling words, spell possessives correctly, analyze word origins and etymologies, and identify misspelled words.

Exercise A You may want to administer a pretest before handing out Spelling Master 8. See Teaching Notes for Spelling Master 1 for instructions.

Exercise B Unscrambling letters to write spelling words is a fun way for students to practice recognizing common letter patterns. If students enjoy this type of activity, encourage them to construct word scrambles with other spelling words to challenge their classmates.

Exercise C To review basic rules for spelling possessives, see pages 746–749 in the Pupil's Edition.

Exercise D To extend this exercise, challenge students to come up with and spell words that share any of the word parts featured in this activity. For example, *exfoliate* also comes from the Latin word *folium*.

Exercise E These items help students learn to identify misspelled words in a list.

SPELLING MASTER 9

In this master, students will write ten new spelling words correctly, identify words based on their shapes, divide words into syllables, analyze the spellings of

words with affixes, and identify spelling errors in sentences.

Exercise A You may want to administer a pretest before handing out Spelling Master 9. See Teaching Notes for Spelling Master 1 for instructions.

Exercise B To model this exercise, choose a spelling word from this master, such as *experiment*, and have students outline the shape of each letter with a box.

Exercise C Remind students that a dictionary is a good resource that shows how words should be divided into syllables. For additional practice dividing words into syllables, see page 765 in the Pupil's Edition.

Exercise D Extend the exercise by having students brainstorm other words with the same prefixes. To review basic rules for spelling words with affixes, see pages 769–771 in the Pupil's Edition.

Exercise E These items help students learn to recognize spelling errors in context.

SPELLING MASTER 10

In this master, students will write ten new spelling words correctly, unscramble letters to write spelling words, spell basic sight words based on their phonetic spellings, analyze word origins and etymologies, and identify spelling errors in sentences.

Exercise A You may want to administer a pretest before handing out Spelling Master 10. See Teaching Notes for Spelling Master 1 for instructions.

Exercise B Unscrambling letters to write spelling words is a fun way for students to practice recognizing common letter patterns. If students enjoy this type of activity, encourage them to create word puzzles with other spelling words to challenge their classmates.

Exercise C Before beginning this activity, have students look up one or two of their spelling words to see how they are represented phonetically. For a sample dictionary entry including pronunciation information, see page 857 in the Pupil's Edition.

Exercise D To extend this exercise, challenge students to come up with and spell words that share any of the word parts featured in this activity. For example, *luxurious* also comes from the Latin word *luxus*.

Exercise E These items help students learn to recognize spelling errors in context.

Answer Keys

READING MASTER 1
1. Beginning poets should first master spelling, grammar, and the various forms of poetry.
2. C
3. B
4. A
5. D

READING MASTER 2
1. Students may say that Black Elk describes his experience in the Wild West Show; they may answer more specifically and say that he describes two meetings with Queen Victoria.
2. B
3. B
4. B
5. A

READING MASTER 3
1. Answers may vary. Students might be able to identify the manatee, or may recognize it generally as an aquatic animal. Other students might discuss their knowledge of mermaids or the Kennedy Space Center.
2. D
3. C
4. B
5. D

READING MASTER 4
1. Answers may vary. Students may say that the author dislikes the jacket's color or style. Other students may say the author is disappointed because it is not like the black leather jacket he describes to his mother.
2. B
3. A
4. C
5. B

READING MASTER 5
1. C
2. Answers may vary.
Visual Details: the black and silver tray of food; the bean soup with white *mochi*, like marshmallows
Sounds: the sounds Mr. Matsui makes; Mother and Father's murmuring
Tastes: the sweet, chocolatey *oshiruko*, the hotly seasoned burdock
Smells: fragrant *nishime*

3. A
4. C
5. B

READING MASTER 6
1. From the illustration and title, students may predict that Coyote will place the stars by using a bow and arrows.
2. A
3. D
4. D
5. C

READING MASTER 7
1. Answers will vary. Students should provide step-by-step instructions for how to eat a certain food.
2. B
3. B
4. C
5. B

READING MASTER 8
1. Students may anticipate that the ad will discuss similarities between bananas and milk. They may look at the small illustration and guess that the ad will promote milk products.
2. B
3. C
4. A
5. A

READING MASTER 9
1. Responses will vary. Annemarie's depiction as a child includes playing with a new kitten and running a race at school. Annemarie's work in the Resistance includes helping a Jewish friend and delivering important packets to a ship captain.
2. D
3. B
4. D
5. B

READING MASTER 10
1. C
2. Responses will vary. The cheetah's speed is similar to cats'; body build is similar to dogs'; dull claws are similar to dogs'; one very sharp claw is similar to cats'.
3. D
4. B
5. D

VOCABULARY MASTER 1

Exercise A Students should copy the words and definitions accurately.

Exercise B
1. exclude: prefix *ex–*, "out" + root *–clude–*, "close." The addition of the prefix *ex–* to the root *–clude–* makes a verb which means "to close out." Excluding something means closing it out or rejecting it.
2. infrequent: prefix *in–*, "not" + root *–frequent–*, "often." The addition of the prefix *in–* to the adjective *frequent* makes an adjective meaning "not frequent," or "seldom."
3. supervise: prefix *super–*, "over" + root *–vise–*, "see." Adding the prefix *super–* to the root *–vise–* makes a verb meaning "to oversee," which is the same as "to direct or manage."

Exercise C
1. anguish
2. infrequent
3. adopt

Exercise D Answers will vary. Students should correctly use all of the assigned words in their reports.

Exercise E
1. D
2. B

VOCABULARY MASTER 2

Exercise A Students should copy the words and definitions accurately.

Exercise B Answers may vary.
1. edible: The parts of the word *edible* literally mean "able to be eaten." The adjective describes things that can be eaten both because they are food and because they are in a state that makes them fit to eat.
2. eloquent: The word *eloquent* now designates someone who not only "speaks out," as its origins suggest, but who also does so in a particularly effective way.
3. offend: To *offend* someone is to "strike against" that person in a way that is not necessarily physical.

Exercise C Answers will vary. Answers should clearly demonstrate the student's understanding of the meanings of the vocabulary words.

Answer Keys *(Continued)*

Exercise D
1. Sentence A is correct.
2. Sentence B is correct.

Exercise E
1. C
2. B

VOCABULARY MASTER 3

Exercise A   Students should copy the words and definitions accurately.

Exercise B   Answers may vary.
1. The prefix *con–* combines with the root *–form–* to make a verb meaning "form together"; to conform is to become the same as something else, and therefore "formed together" with it.
2. The root *–gramma–* combines with the suffixes *–atic* and *–al* to make an adjective describing something "of or like something written."
3. The root *–grat–* combines with the suffix *–fy* to make a verb meaning "to cause to feel pleased."

Exercise C   Wording of definitions will vary.
1. manual: adjective; using the hands
2. conforms: verb; agrees with; is in compliance with
3. impact: noun; effect
4. modest: adjective; humble; not overly grand

Exercise D
1. Definition 2 is correct.
2. Definition 1 is correct.

Exercise E
1. C
2. D

VOCABULARY MASTER 4

Exercise A   Students should copy the words and definitions accurately.

Exercise B
1. veto: from the Latin word *vetare*, "to forbid." A veto is an order that forbids something.
2. aggravate: from the Latin word *aggravare*, "to make heavier." To aggravate a problem or situation makes it seem more burdensome, or heavier.
3. distort: from the Latin prefix *dis–*, an intensifier, and the Latin word *torquere*, "to twist." When something is distorted, it is twisted.

4. recognition: from the Latin prefix *re–*, "again," and the Latin word *cognoscere*, "to know." Every time you see something that you recognize, in a sense you "know it again."

Exercise C
1. confirm
2. irritable
3. aggravated

Exercise D   Answers may vary.
1. commitment
2. comparison
3. compare
4. ignore
5. ignorant

Exercise E
1. B
2. A

VOCABULARY MASTER 5

Exercise A   Students should copy the words and definitions accurately.

Exercise B   Answers may vary.
1. loiter: from the Dutch word *leuteren*, "to dawdle." The word has the same meaning in both languages.
2. myth: from the Greek word *mythos*, meaning "a word, speech, story, or legend." The word *myth* now usually designates traditional stories such as those in Greek and Roman mythology.
3. satellite: from the French word *satellite*. The word has the same meaning in both languages.
4. camouflage: from the French word *camoufler*, "to disguise." Camouflage is a disguise that helps something or someone to blend in with the surroundings.

Exercise C   Answers will vary.
Possible associations:
1. ridiculed: pain, embarrassment
2. tranquil: peaceful, restfulness, quiet
3. myth: untruth, fantasy
4. loiter: hanging around, wasting time

Exercise D   Answers will vary. Students should correctly use all of the assigned words in their letters.

Exercise E
1. B
2. B

VOCABULARY MASTER 6

Exercise A   Students should copy the words and definitions accurately.

Exercise B   Answers may vary.
1. The prefix *manu–* combines with the root *–script–* to make a noun designating something that is "written by hand." Originally, the word *manuscript* applied only to handwritten work.
2. In this word, *geo–* is a prefix that combines with the root *–logy–* to make a noun meaning "science of the earth." The addition of the suffix *–ical* forms an adjective meaning "having to do with the science of the earth."
3. The prefix *sub–* combines with the root *–merg–* to make an adjective meaning "plunged under"; the suffix *–ed* indicates an adjective formed from a verb.

Exercise C
1. stationary
2. duel
3. kernel
4. faze

Exercise D   Answers will vary. Answers should clearly demonstrate the student's understanding of the meanings of the vocabulary words.

Exercise E
1. D
2. C

VOCABULARY MASTER 7

Exercise A   Students should copy the words and definitions accurately.

Exercise B   Students' sentences should accurately use each of the specialized terms. Definitions:
1. refrain (music): a phrase or verse that is repeated periodically throughout a song or poem
2. magnitude (astronomy): the brightness of a celestial body
3. overture (music): a musical introduction to a larger musical work

Exercise C   Answers will vary. Students should correctly use all of the assigned words in their letters.

Answer Keys (Continued)

Exercise D
1. Sentence A is correct.
2. Sentence A is correct.

Exercise E
1. C
2. B

VOCABULARY MASTER 8

Exercise A   Students should copy the words and definitions accurately.

Exercise B
1. maternal: root *–mater–*, "mother" + suffix *–al*, "of or like." The addition of *–al* to *–mater–* results in the adjective *maternal,* describing something or someone "of or like a mother."
2. revise: prefix *re–*, "again" + root *–vise–*, "see." The prefix and root make a verb which means "to see again"; when revising something, you must be able to see it again objectively to determine what changes you should make.
3. indispensable: prefix *in–*, "not" + root *–dispense–* "do away with" + suffix *–able*, "able." The combination of the root and affixes results in an adjective describing something that "cannot be dispensed with."

Exercise C   Answers will vary. Possible associations:
1. hysterical: extreme excitement, surprise
2. maternal: caring, loving, nurturing feelings
3. prestige: vanity, a desire for attention, fame

Exercise D
1. capacity
2. indispensable
3. pivoted
4. hysterical
5. illustrious

Exercise E
1. A
2. C

VOCABULARY MASTER 9

Exercise A   Students should copy the words and definitions accurately.

Exercise B
1. vital: from the Latin word *vita,* "life." *Vital* originally meant "essential to life," but now can describe anything which is considered indispensable.
2. avert: from the Latin prefix *a–*, "from," and the Latin word *vertere,* "to turn." To avert something means to turn it away and keep it from happening.
3. patron: from the Latin word *patronus,* "a protector or defender." The meaning of *patron* has expanded to indicate a person who helps and supports another person or group in various ways, not just by physical defense or protection.
4. inferior: from the Latin word *inferus,* "low, below." Something inferior is low in importance or quality.

Exercise C   Answers may vary.
1. fascination
2. fascinating
3. invasion
4. expansion
5. expandable

Exercise D   Answers will vary. Answers should clearly demonstrate the student's understanding of the meanings of the vocabulary words.

Exercise E
1. D
2. B

VOCABULARY MASTER 10

Exercise A   Students should copy the words and definitions accurately.

Exercise B   Answers may vary.
1. The prefix *zo–* combines with the root *–logy–* to make a noun meaning "the science of animals."
2. The root *–leg–* combines with the suffix *–ible* to make an adjective meaning "that which can be read," or "readable."
3. The combination of the root *–toler–* and the suffix *–able* make an adjective meaning "bearable"; the addition of the prefix *in–* makes the adjective mean "not bearable."
4. The suffix *–ity* combines with the root *–velox–* to make a noun meaning "swiftness" or "speed."

Exercise C   Answers may vary.
1. under + growth: *Undergrowth* is a collective word for all the plants and small trees that "grow under" the taller trees of a forest.
2. self + conscious: *Self-conscious* means to be overly aware or conscious of one's self—one's appearance, actions, or speech.

Exercise D   Answers will vary. Students' answers should demonstrate their understanding of the meanings of the vocabulary words.

Exercise E
1. B
2. C

SPELLING MASTER 1

Exercise A   Students should copy the words accurately.

Exercise B   acceptance, again, careless, existence, instead

Exercise C
1. for / eign
2. com / mit / tee
3. vil / lain
4. nine / ty

Exercise D
1. acceptance, accept, no change
2. existence, exist, no change
3. careless, care, no change
4. ninety, nine, no change

Exercise E
1. B
2. C

SPELLING MASTER 2

Exercise A   Students should copy the words accurately.

Exercise B
1. genius
2. treasury
3. favorite
4. decision

Exercise C
1. bicycles, add *–s*
2. countries, change *y* to *ie* and add *–s*
3. decisions, add *–s*
4. geniuses, add *–es*
5. treasuries, change *y* to *ie* and add *–s*

Answer Keys (Continued)

Exercise D
1. bicycle
2. bouquet
3. sympathy
4. suspicion
5. sense

Exercise E
1. C
2. B
3. A

SPELLING MASTER 3

Exercise A Students should copy the words accurately.

Exercise B accumulate, argument conscious, doesn't, jealous, nervous, realize

Exercise C
1. can't
2. doesn't
3. don't
4. won't

Exercise D Answers may vary.
1. –ative; argumentative; no change
2. –ness; consciousness; no change
3. –y; jealousy; no change
4. –ly; nervously; no change
5. –ation; realization; drop –*e*

Exercise E
1. D
2. B

SPELLING MASTER 4

Exercise A Students should copy the words accurately.

Exercise B acquire, across, brief, control, criticize, extremely, interpret, privilege, speech, strength

Exercise C
1. brief
2. privilege
3. across
4. criticize
5. acquire

Exercise D
1. interpret
2. extremely
3. control
4. strength
5. speech

Exercise E
1. B
2. A

SPELLING MASTER 5

Exercise A Students should copy the words accurately.

Exercise B
1. apparent
2. occasion
3. audience
4. judgment
5. temperament

Exercise C
1. ap / par / ent
2. can / di / date
3. ef / fi / cien / cy
4. judg / ment
5. oc / ca / sion

Exercise D
1. candidate
2. personal
3. correspondence
4. fortunately
5. audience

Exercise E
1. B
2. B

SPELLING MASTER 6

Exercise A Students should copy the words accurately.

Exercise B bough, cough, straight, though, through, throughout, tonight

Exercise C
1. whose
2. cough
3. throughout
4. straight
5. tonight

Exercise D
1. bough
2. bow
3. Who's
4. whose
5. threw; through

Exercise E
1. D
2. A

SPELLING MASTER 7

Exercise A Students should copy the words accurately.

Exercise B perceive, receive, university, unnecessary

Exercise C
1. mischief
2. describe
3. interest
4. definite
5. perceive

Exercise D
transferred; university; mischief; unnecessary; perceive

Exercise E
1. B
2. C

SPELLING MASTER 8

Exercise A Students should copy the words accurately.

Exercise B
1. rhythm
2. foliage
3. friend
4. muscle
5. heir

Exercise C
1. rhythm's
2. friend's; women's
3. heir's; attorney's
4. February's; icicles'
5. society's

Exercise D
1. society
2. foliage
3. muscle
4. icicles
5. women

Exercise E
1. B
2. C

SPELLING MASTER 9

Exercise A Students should copy the words accurately.

Exercise B
1. description
2. independent
3. mathematics
4. repetition
5. performance

Exercise C
1. ex / act / ly
2. ex / per / i / ment
3. per / form / ance
4. per / ma / nent
5. un / u / su / al / ly

Answer Keys *(Continued)*

Exercise D
1. independent, depend, no change
2. uncomfortable, comfort, no change
3. unusually, usual, no change

Exercise E
1. A
2. B

SPELLING MASTER 10

Exercise A Students should copy the words accurately.

Exercise B
1. aisles
2. ceiling
3. technique
4. fierce
5. imaginary

Exercise C
1. vague
2. luxury
3. minute
4. hungrily

Exercise D
1. familiar
2. aisles
3. luxury
4. fierce
5. ceiling

Exercise E
1. A
2. B

PRACTICE TEST 1
Part 1: Reading Comprehension
1. B
2. D
3. C
4. A
5. C

Part 2: Vocabulary
6. D
7. A
8. B
9. C
10. D
11. D
12. A
13. B
14. C
15. B

Part 3: Spelling
16. A
17. B
18. B
19. C
20. D
21. D
22. A
23. B
24. C
25. B

PRACTICE TEST 2
Part 1: Reading Comprehension
1. C
2. B
3. D
4. C
5. A

Part 2: Vocabulary
6. D
7. B
8. A
9. C
10. B
11. B
12. C
13. D
14. A
15. B

Part 3: Spelling
16. C
17. B
18. C
19. B
20. D
21. C
22. A
23. D
24. C
25. D